UP

GO

CAN

YOU

Concerned Publications, Inc.
Box 1024
Clermont, Florida 32711

Copyright © 1984 by William And DeLoras Stringfellow

Library of Congress Cataloging in Publication Data

ISBN 0-939286-03-3

Printed in the United States of America

With deepest appreciation
to Herb and Rowena Rogers,
two individuals who have
found *"The Critical Concept"*
and are taking it as high as
possible in their lives.

CONTENTS

CHAPTER ONE
THE TRAP

The statistics indicate that there are only two groups. There is eighty-one percent in one group and just nineteen percent in the other.

One of those who made up the eighty-one percent attracted quite a crowd. As a matter of fact, they pushed and shoved to get a glimpse of him. Some stood on tip-toes in front of the twenty-two story building trying to see.

Blue police car lights danced unevenly with the red ones from the ambulance, and bounced off the brick wall.

A blanket-covered stretcher carried the lifeless body up and into the ambulance. The by-standers covered their ears as the siren blasted out the news that the ambulance wanted a clearance in the blocked traffic.

A crimson red puddle on the sidewalk told the gruesome story. A man had jumped out of one of the top floor windows!

After the crowd had gone, the isolated figure of a man was seen going to and from the spot where the body had hit the pavement with a thud. He just could not imagine anyone doing such a horrible thing. His curiosity made him ask several bystanders who it was. No one knew. Neither the security guard nor the maintenance man could reveal his identity.

Going from floor to floor, office to office, from the top floor downward, the concerned stranger finally discovered that it had been a clerk in the insurance company that occupied the entire sixteenth floor who had made that fatal leap. As work had almost come to a halt, further inquiries were made easier.

Strangely, none of the employees really knew him. Sure, he was quiet, polite, a hard worker and all that, but no one seemed to know much about his personal life.

Reading the short obituary notice just did not answer the plaguing question of why a man would jump out of the window and kill himself. So, he attended the graveside funeral. The minister did not help much with his memorized message. One or two of those who paid their last respects gave him a little information, but just enough to increase the tormenting curiosity.

The neighbors were responsive to his probings, and a few more pieces were placed in the puzzle.

The stock market had not inspired a depressed buyer's plunge.

There had been no romantic rejection by a lover.

No clandestine affair.

No missing or misused company funds.

No doctor's damning cancer report.

There was absolutely no apparent cause for suicide.

Nothing!

Forty-nine years, eleven months and twenty-nine days. One more day and the man would have had a birthday cake and ice cream awaiting him as he came into his house sharply at 5:56 P.M.

The insurance clerk had left home every day, five days a week, at 7:38 A.M., arriving a few minutes before everyone else. His coffee breaks were taken at his desk in an unceremonial fashion with a nine-year old thermos bottle.

At 12:00 sharp, he left his desk, walked to the elevator, pushed the "down" button, and stepped off onto the second floor. Turning left, he had walked to the small coffee shop tucked in one corner. Even though the vendor offered a small variety of hot and cold drinks, he had always preferred lemonade in the spring and summer, and hot chocolate in the fall and winter.

5:00 each afternoon found him back on the elevator with five or six others, going down.

Almost mechanically, he found practically the same seat on the bus that became crowded in four or five stops after picking him up. There were exactly 652 steps from the bus stop to his yard, and 39 more to his front door.

Day in, and day out, the routine was the same.

Weekends were spent either washing the four-year old station wagon, raking leaves from the neighbors' oak trees, mowing the 75' × 110' yard that had failed to produce a thick, plush, green lawn, or shoveling snow from the walk and driveway.

His sporting interests were confined to those events he viewed on t.v.

He had provided the necessities for his wife

and children. He had made a few bank loans to help the two daughters and one son obtain a college degree. The loans necessitated his wearing the same plain and inexpensive clothes long after their style and usefulness had passed.

The children had all married and moved away. Even though one daughter was expecting a child, there were no grandchildren's pictures adorning the mantle of the small fireplace in the modest frame home.

The children did not visit nor write very often.

"Nothing" caused his successful suicide attempt.

Tony's story was just the opposite. That is why he has been placed in the nineteen percent bracket.

Tony was an immigrant from Sicily. He could speak very little English, and could read just a slight bit more. Consequently, he found it very difficult to get work. Like the average person, he went from store to store asking if they needed any help. For several weeks, as his meager funds diminished rapidly, he continued the hard task of asking almost everyone he met if they knew of anyone who was hiring. The answers were always negative. Yet, he continued to plod along, hoping that the next day would bring his breakthrough.

One day he noticed a sign in the window of a busy restaurant. He asked a passerby what the sign read. He was told that the restaurant wanted to hire a bookkeeper.

He went into the restaurant and asked to see the owner. When the owner came Tony asked how much he paid for a "keeper of books." The owner, looking at his ragged, foreign clothes, told him, "I'm afraid you've made a mistake. We're looking for someone who can do accounting. You don't look like someone who can manage the records of our financial dealings."

Before leaving he turned around and asked the owner, "How much does this keeper of the books get paid?"

The man kindly replied, "About eighty-five dollars a week."

Eighty-five dollars seemed like a large fortune when he thought about the fact that he had as his total net worth two dimes!

Passing a small fruit stand, he decided to invest one of the dimes in his survival. The large, red, Delicious brand apples were just 5¢ each. By eating one a day, he could survive two days for ten cents. Since they were not too clean, he started polishing one with his colorful bandana-handkerchief he had brought with him from the old country. Overcome with hunger he finally sat down on the curb. Not realizing that he was in the heart of the business district, he took the highly polished apple out of his oversized jacket and placed it on the curb next to his body. Then he took the other apple and slowly began to polish it, trying all the time to decide which one he would eat. In a moment, a hand reached down and grasped the apple. He grabbed the hand to get back his apple, when the person placed a quarter in his lap. He released his death grip and looked up at the well-dressed man.

"Those surely are beautiful apples you're selling, friend. Is a quarter enough?"

"Yah, yah, tank you," he stuttered.

Before he could analyze this amazing incident, another man took his other apple, leaving a second quarter.

As he sat there still dazed by what had happened to him in less than three minutes, he felt rich! He had fifty cents! With only a ten cent investment, he had gone into business for himself! And that is exactly what he did!

Returning to the fruit stand some ten blocks away, he asked in his broken English how many apples could he get for fifty cents. The proprietor, himself being an immigrant, gave him twelve apples for fifty cents, a bonus of two apples.

He rushed back to that magical spot in the downtown business section, got out his handkerchief, and began polishing apples. Before noon, he had sold all twelve apples, realizing a total income of $3.00. In his excitement, he forgot his own hunger. He purchased $3.00 worth of apples and returned to his own private fruit stand on the corner. By the end of that business day, he had sold all his apples except one. He ate that one as his reward for success.

Bright and early the next morning he was waiting for the fruit stand owner to arrive and open for business. As he told of his success, the proprietor took him inside and they sat down on two empty apple crates.

"Listen," he said with an understanding smile, "You've got enough money to go to the wholesaler and buy a whole crate of apples at a much cheaper price."

Following his new found friend's advice, he sought and found the wholesale produce market, secured a crate of apples, and went back down-town to peddle his fruit.

After successfully selling his apples for three weeks, he was ordered to leave. Yet, this did not daunt his spirits. He secured a child's old wagon at a pawn shop and began to pull be-hind him through the residential areas a crate of apples along with an additional line of ba-nanas and grapes.

Within a short time he found a much larger cart with bicycle wheels and tires that pulled much easier. Every day he could be seen tug-ging away at the cart as he yelled out, "Bananas, apples, and grapes!"

A relative came to the United States five months after he had started peddling his fruit up and down the streets. Tony gave him his wagon, some fruit and a lesson in making change, then Tony bought a newer cart for himself, making his business double.

Five years after that first apple was pur-chased from the red, white and blue scarf, Tony opened up his own wholesale fruit business, selling to retail stores all over the county. Within fifteen years after arriving in America, Tony had married another Sicilian immigrant, was the father of seven boys and one girl, and lived in a very fashionable section of town.

One day he decided to go to the bank and make a loan with which to build his own mod-ern building. As he was explaining to the bank's vice-president why he wanted the loan, the vice-president commented on how much the bank appreciated his business and how he felt there would be no problem in their making the loan. The vice-president drew up the papers and asked Tony to read them.

"I'm a sorry," Tony said, "I donna read mucha English."

"You mean to tell me that you have had such tremendous success in your own business and you can't read," the executive said in absolute amazement. "Tell me," he asked very sincerely, "where would you be right now if you could read?"

"Oh, that's a easy," Tony said with a big smile, "I'd be an $85.00 a week bookkeeper!"

Both Tony and the insurance clerk, strange as it may seem, had one thing in common. They both had "time."

Time. There is a strange paradox about time. It drags like a snail when you are waiting for someone, yet it flies when you are dashing to the airport before the plane leaves.

When a person is twelve years old, "Dad's" thirty-eight years seem to be millenniums away. Yet, at thirty-eight, twelve seems as if it were just yesterday.

Time not only plays tricks on the mind, it also is guilty of grand theft. Time steals away potentials and successes. It robs men and women of fulfilled dreams. It swindles humans of satisfaction. Time slips up from behind and pickpockets the would-be succeeder. No wonder one man said that "wasted time is wasted life."

Time also changes concepts.

A young couple stands before the officiating minister with after-wedding visions of love, romance, joy, and excitement. The bride sees a rambling, white, colonial home with a black roof and matching shutters. A carpet of plush, green grass surrounds the home. Bright red roses line the wide, brick driveway. Children are playing pirates as they climb up a rope ladder to their secret hide-a-way in the largest of the twenty oak trees that nearly cover the five acre homesite with a blanket of shade.

The groom sees a lemon-yellow convertable with wire wheels and a turbo diesel engine that is almost dwarfed by the fifteen passenger, tinted window van parked beside it in front of the two car garage. He also pictures gold leaf letters on the mahogany door to the penthouse office spelling out his name with "President" beneath it.

Sinister time creeps in, and the vision has become a three bedroom, one and a half bath, concrete block home on a 90′ × 110′ combined patch of grass, stickers and sand.

The children, grown and married, live hundreds of miles away. Thoughts now center around the seven long years before retirement. The visions portray a pension and social security checks to buy and operate that nice motor home in which they can "see the U.S.A." in comfort.

The annual arrivals of "baby time", and the equal number of departures of "father time" see the dreams of travel now limited to overcoming the obstacles in listening to blaring car horns announcing that reflexes and driving skills have slowed considerably. The comfortable "Golden Years" have surrendered to pain; and survival is the name of the game.

As the funeral service has ended with the lowering of that mate's body into its resting

place, lonely days and sleepless nights plague
the survivor. Then, within a few months, the
survivor succumbs.

Speeding time pauses long enough to an-
nounce that someone else never found the secret of living life at its best. Another individual
in the eighty-one percent group!

Another person caught in the trap!

CHAPTER TWO
THE ILLUSIVE DREAM

It was one of the most luxurious motor homes made. It had everything in it, including the kitchen sink. Even the driver could flip a switch and immediately get a picture on the dashboard t.v. screen of the area behind the motor home. This way he could see clearly before backing up.

On the rear of this beautiful home-on-wheels was a large chrome bumper. On the bumper was a heavy plastic sign which carried these words: "Pay your taxes promptly; I need my Social Security check."

Bumper stickers, or as Paul Harvey calls them, "Bumper Snickers," are seen everywhere. Many are humorous. Many are serious. Some are immoral, but most are moral. Over and over again, there is one theme portrayed on the bumpers of cars, vans, and trucks. It goes like this:

"Happiness is having a clean Volkswagen."

"Happiness is owning a warm puppy."

"Happiness is having the family home in the evenings."

Happiness is the singular, most sought after

17

goal today. Everyone wants to find happiness, and the ways and means people employ in their mad pursuit of happiness can actually boggle the mind.

This story is told in another book, but it is so meaningful that you should see it on these pages: A certain regular business men's meeting had a much different program this time. Each member had been given a small piece of paper and a pencil. Instead of the normal after-dinner speaker the program chairman for that meeting brought ten well dressed men into the restaurant's convention hall and had them stand on a slightly elevated platform. The members were asked to look the ten men over very carefully, and to write down their impressions.

Of the one hundred and twenty-two men and ladies who wrote down the first thing that came to their minds no two club members came up with the same impression. There were one hundred and twenty-two different written statements.

The insurance executive saw ten large life insurance policies. The evangelical minister invisioned ten strong laymen for his church. The Air Force officer thought about ten recruits for officer's candiate school. The single secretary saw ten eligible bachelors. Ten men and one hundred and twenty-two evaluations.

Now the irony of it all is that these ten men turned out to be convicts! They were out of prison for the day to lecture high school students about the foolishness of crime.

Now, by the same token, place 100 people—men, ladies, and young people—before you and ask them to write down briefly what they each believe happiness is.

You know what will result, don't you? Only this time there will not be 100 different answers. They will fall into several basic catagories.

First, and not necessarily in importance, will be wealth. This word, "wealth," or its companions, "riches," "a fortune," "affluence," and "financially-fixed" are held up as the answer to all of life's problems.

A certain baby was born in the northwest section of Texas in a seldom heard of place called Canadian. When the 1929 stock market crash came, this man, who had studied for about two years at the University of Virginia, started building a large fortune by short-selling stocks. After a complicated legal battle in the 1940's, he gained control of the Allegheny Corporation, a holding company for the Chesapeake & Ohio, the Pere Marquette, the Nickel Plate, and other railroads.

In 1942, he became board chairman of the Chesapeake and Ohio, and in 1952 of the New York Central.

Yet, with an estimated 1958 estate of eight and one half million dollars, which would be possibly four to five times that valuable today, Mr. Robert Young took his own life in his luxurious Palm Beach mansion.

The statistics concerning suicides, and suicidal attempts, among the wealthiest individuals in our country alone would boggle the mind. Those same startling figures also spell out the fact that money and possessions, by themselves, cannot bring any individual true happiness.

Second, and again not necessarily in order of

importance, many individuals would state that
happiness is truly being healthy.

This common belief is vividly being acted
out in the overwhelming attendance at health
clubs, gyms, and exercise classes. Just a few
short years ago, anyone seen running down
the street would have been thought of as some
petty thief running away from the police. It
would not surprise many people to soon see
city, county and state highway department
crews out along the roads erecting yellow signs
portraying a human being in a running position,
with the words beneath it, "Caution, joggers
ahead."

At one time people would have stared from
car and home windows at an elderly couple
walking down a sidewalk at a fast pace. Now,
particularly in the winter months in Florida,
Southern California, and Arizona, it is a common sight for even the very, very elderly to be
attired in bright red, white and blue exercise
suits, beating florescent-colored sneakers down
on the pavement at a rapid pace.

The desire to remain healthy extends from
exercise to the also multi-billion dollar phar-
maceutical business to the astronomical hospi-
tal/physician drain on the economy. To main-
tain health has almost become such an obsession
that it even goes far beyond addiction.

Yet, if happiness were to be found in being
healthy, then every person who passes his or
her physical would be happy. And it doesn't
require a doctor's degree in medicine or psychi-
atry to see that it just doesn't work that way.

Third, many feel that happiness can be acquired through fame. In 1903, a baby with the

first name of Leslie and the middle name of Townes, born in England, did not seem to have the requirements for attaining fame. Moving to Cleveland, Ohio, he slowly began to feel the need of happiness in a strange manner. In 1933 he tried to satisfy that desire for fame by performing in vaudeville with a rapid-fire delivery of jokes. In 1933 he starred in the musical "Roberta." In 1962 Congress voted him a gold medal. He wrote two autobiographies, "They've Got Me Covered," and "Have Tux, Will Travel."

Leslie Townes Hope has traveled millions of miles, entertaining military men in several wars, as well as in the peaceful times in between. He made several films with the famous Bing Crosby (which almost became synonymous with the two of them).

Bob Hope's wealth is exaggerated on his own shows; yet, it is so vast that he could spend more each day than the average American's salary and hardly make a dent in his total estate.

If fame, in itself, brought true happiness, Bob Hope's biography would not portray him as the most traveled, most performed comedian in history.

Neither would American history books contain the tragic entries of famed people like Judy Garland, Marilyn Monroe, and others who took their own lives.

Fourth, many feel that marriage will bring about real happiness. It is a known fact that in practically every case of worry and fear of some calamity or catastrophe, "the anticipation is greater than the realization." The problem generally is exaggerated out of proportion to the actual thing itself. As it has been said many times, "Nothing is as bad as it seems."

Tragically, but true, it is the same with marriage. If the majority of marriages are ending up in divorce courts and a large percentage of the balance are "fighting it out to the bitter end," can this be the panacea, the cure-all for unhappiness?

Tommy Manville, the asbestos king with a twenty million dollar estate to his acclaim, set the record for "millionaire divorces." Thirteen times to be exact! His seventh marriage lasted exactly seven and one half HOURS!

Marriage, in itself, does not capture that illusive creature called Happiness.

Some people feel that travel really brings happiness. Today, a certain group of people have funds with which to do a great deal of globe-trotting. In their unusual, and many times extravagant, jaunts across the ocean to foreign countries, they have acquired the slang title of "the jet-set."

A close observation of the habits, personalities, and characteristics of these jet-setters will reveal just the opposite of the theory that cruising creates contentment.

The private lives of so many of these on-the-move nobilities are actually an exposé of pathetic sadness and sorrow. Too many times they are like the wife of the poor laborer when a small circus was set up in the field across from his humble home.

It was exciting for the man, his wife, and small son to sit on the front porch in the late afternoon after work and watch the workmen start to erect the ferris wheel, merry-go-round, bumper-cars, side shows, games, and attractions. Then came the crowds from nearby small towns. Evening after evening they watched the different cars pull into the parking lot, the people enter the front gate, and dash off to a night of fun. Once or twice, they ate their evening meal on their laps so they would not miss the excitement and constant activities.

Several nights they fell asleep watching from their bedroom windows the bright lights flashing off and on, up and down, in and around.

Then came the last night.

The wife told her husband that she and their child were going to walk across the street and go in. He declined, but they went anyway. After a couple of hours, he decided to go, too. When he found his wife and son, they told him that they had just been walking all around. They had not bought anything or gone on any rides. "But," she said with a big smile, "We're both going to go on the merry-go-round."

"You don't have any money," he replied.

"Yes, I do," she said with an even bigger grin, "I washed two of the circus wagons today. I got a whole dollar!"

"Well, how much does it cost to ride on it?" he asked.

"Fifty cents! And Little Charles and I are a-fixing to get on it."

Soon, the two of them had purchased their tickets, climbed up on two horses, side by side, and were slowly starting to move. Big Charles stood and watched. In a few seconds the merry-go-round had brought them slowly around in front of him again. The two waved and he waved back. Then the ride became faster and

faster. Up and down the horses would go, with
them waving and laughing all the time.

The machine slowly came to a halt along
with the music, and everyone climbed off and
down onto the ground. The small family of
three were united again. As they walked out of
the grounds and back toward their home, the
husband did not smile or say a word. The wife
noticed that something was wrong.

After Little Charles was fast asleep, the two
of them made their way to their own bed. She
asked him what was wrong. And he replied,
"Well, I think it's a sin!"

"What's a sin?"

"Well, I'll tell you. I think it's a sin what you
done tonight. You worked hard washing them
wagons, didn't you?"

"I guess it was a little hard," she said in a
subdued manner, "why?"

"Well, you went over there with Little Charles
and got on that merry-go-round and spent it
all. You went up and down, and round and
round. Now you're broke and you're right back
where you started from!"

Happiness is not found in any of these things,
in and by themselves. And in most cases, it is
not to be had by the accumulation of all of
them. Nevertheless, happiness can be found
today. But before you can even begin to have a
hint of it, several things must happen in your
life. Please notice the last sentence very, very
carefully and look closely at one two-lettered
word. Do not think the word is "it." No, to the
contrary, "it" isn't it! The word is the 17th. in
that sentence. The word is "in." The sentence
reads, "But before you can even begin to have

a hint of it [happiness], several things must happen *in* your life."

First, you have to discover that nineteen percent group. And, second, understand how one gets there. Then, third, utilize the unique concept to all its dynamic potential in your life.

CHAPTER THREE
ONLY A SELECT FEW?

Psychiatrists and psychologists are backed up in their findings by front-line employment counselors who firmly believe that those two groups make up the eighty-one percent and the nineteen percent.

That is, they are persuaded that eighty-one percent of all the work force, blue and white collar alike, are unhappy with what they are doing!

Not only are 81% of all men and women dissatisfied with their occupations and vocations, but with life in general!

Add to that the fact that the majority of the 81% feel that they are in a trap. Pile on one more statistic and the picture grows even more grim. A large percentage of this staggering number of sincere human beings do not really see much hope for a sensational, life-altering tomorrow. They do not see any way out of their present situation or position in life.

What makes this so terrible is that all this is happening right in the middle of the most educated, scientific, cultured society in existence!

No one seems to really know what prompted

the killing of John Fitzgerald Kennedy in Dallas, Texas in 1963. Millions recognize that it was a great loss. Yet, the largest portion of the very ones who cannot comprehend this tremendous loss, cannot perceive an even greater waste of life . . . their own.

Kennedy could not keep that bullet from destroying his future, but you can learn the forces at work that place those 81% in that crippling catagory. Also, you can comprehend how to join the 19% and how that power can not only keep you out of the pit, but can help you truly go up!

Consider something else.

Despite the great emphasis on health today, despite the innumerable spas, exercise classes, gyms, and physical fitness facilities finding an overwhelming interest and participation, and despite the tremendous and widely varied recreational activities available to the average citizen, and despite the large, large number of men and women flocking to them, there is still that "morning-after." The "morning-after"—cold, stark, reality of unhappiness and dissatisfaction that seems to strike once again to offset the previous week-end's fast-fleeting pleasures and retreats. "Blue Monday" did not get that name for nothing! There is no way, it seems, to stop that slow, but insidious, sinking feeling as the new week at work starts to bring back the fact that this is not what they really want out of life.

But. . . .

What about that nineteen percent?

How is it that such a small few break through the "tangled web?"

How do they hear a different drummer?

What causes them to rise above their environment?

Where do they find that illusive power to take charge of their lives?

What makes them move ahead of the masses?

How are they able to grab most of the gusto?

What enables them to be all they can be?

Has some Supernatural Power ordained that only a select few will master life?

Or, have these unique individuals discovered some secret formula and drunk deep of its powerful potion?

Are these men and women in this exclusive club endowed with sharper minds, keener wits, better insights, more common sense, greater drives, and increased energies? Have they simply carried these attributes to their natural fulfillments?

Somehow, they seem to have found something that evades the majority.

What is their secret?

Have these happy, successful individuals simply developed certain personal and professional qualities to the place where they stand out above all the rest, and thereby become leaders in their field? Is it just a matter of making themselves over to become what they have seen in other highly productive people?

By some long-shot possibility, could it be that it is not just the development of qualities thay already possessed, but the control of the defects in their character?

No sensible person would give in to the temptation right here to say, "Oh, they were just lucky," or "they were just at the right place at the right time," or "If I had rich and influential parents as they did, I could have done anything I wanted to, too."

Time and history have proved that "being born with a silver spoon in your mouth" doesn't insure success, peace, or happiness any more than being born in a bakery makes you a cinnamon bun.

What you are about to discover has been right at your fingertips all your life. It is a concrete concept that hundreds and hundreds have found to be thrilling and super-satisfying. Almost anyone can be happy, involved, relevant, productive, healthy, and secure, right in the middle of the most commercialized, high pressured, pill-prone society ever known in the history of this planet. Anyone, that is, who can come to an understanding of the cause and effects of this concept.

Thousands have discovered this gold mine and have dug deep into it. Thousands have carried off real riches in self-confidence, powerful persuasion, masterful self-motivation, financial security, and greater enjoyment in life.

Yet, the vein still holds so much, much more for all who want it and will work with it.

You want all these things, and much, much more, don't you? Well, discover the basic laws that either place one in that eighty-one percent pit or helps pull him or her out and up into that nineteen percent tower of fulfillment and happiness.

The balloon salesman, even though he was not aware of it, came close to the exciting comprehension of the concept.

He had his air tank, plywood box of balloons, and a bag of string all strategically placed so that everyone going in, or coming out of the amusement park could see the many colors of balloons he had to offer.

Periodically, he would let go of his hold on one of the balloon strings and it would slowly, but conspicuously, rise up into the sky. And, of course, business would temporarily pick up.

Standing nearby, but not too close to be a nuisance, was a small Negro boy. After watching the salesman release a yellow balloon, then later a red one, and then a blue one, and then a yellow one again, he waited until no one was around and walked over to the aged man.

"Sir," he asked in a soft and polite voice, "If you had a black balloon, would it go up like the others?"

The man bent down closer to the obviously concerned lad, smiled, and said, "Son, it's not the color, but what's inside that makes 'em go up."

When a careful analysis is made of the ones who make up the nineteen percent group of true succeeders, it is seen that neither color, sex, nationality, education, nor background has any bearing on those "going up." None of these externals which many feel are vital requirements for success is necessary. It is "what's inside!"

And once you reach the place where you not only understand the concept that changes "what's inside" and begin to utilize it properly, you, too, will start going up.

A very well known psychologist once said, "An individual's self-concept is the core of his or her personality. It affects every aspect of humans behavior: the ability to learn, the capacity to grow and change, the choice of friends, mates and careers. It's no exaggeration to say that a strong positive self-image is the best possible preparation for success in life."

Why is it that just a microscopically small percentage of human beings, male and female, have such good self-images?

Why is it that this tiny minority of men and women possess healthy self-concepts that everyone else truly envies and tries to emulate?

By the same token, why is it that the largest majority, the eighty-one percent, have such bad self-images? Why is it that almost every single individual, except the nineteen percent group, possesses unhealthy self-concepts?

A certain famous man might well give you some rich revelations.

CHAPTER FOUR
THE ENDOWMENT

You can probably see him now just as clearly and concisely as if he were right there before you. He is probably still the same in your mental picture right now as he was when you first saw him.

You weren't the only one who saw him. Millions saw him, too. They were so impressed with him that they sat around in their living rooms and watched his performance the second time as it came over television.

He is Charlton Heston. He was masterfully portraying the majestic Moses for Cecil B. DeMille's immortal motion picture version of THE TEN COMMANDMENTS.

Whether or not you believe in the Bible, history authenticates the Bible story of Moses. What you cannot read in the Biblical account, or see in the movie, is the fact that from all rights, Moses should never have been the successful leader of an entire nation moving out from slavery in Egypt and into their own tax-free endowment in the Promised Land.

Moses had been a "marked man," so to speak, at birth. All of the male slave babies were to be killed because of the fury of the Egyptian king who gave the orders. Yet, in spite of the odds, Moses was placed in a small cradle made waterproof by pitch, sent down the river under the watchful eye of his sister, and landed right in the arms of the King's daughter, the princess. Falling madly in love with the infant, the childless princess asked Miriam, Moses' sister, if she knew of a good Hebrew mother who would take care of the babe for her. Of course, Moses wound up right back where he started from, in the tender, loving care of his own mother.

He grew into adulthood with all of the wealth of Egypt at his disposal and for his own pleasure as the next ruler. Shortly after becoming forty years of age, a time when most men have become "locked in" to some position or occupational trade, Moses took a ride out into the slave district, where the Hebrews were building the store-cities of Pithom and Raamses. During his inspection tour, he saw an Egyptian knock a Hebrew to the ground. Moses was infuriated, and making sure no one was watching, he killed the Egyptian and buried his body in the sand. But his murder was seen and Moses fled for his life into the Arabian desert land of Midian.

Then, when the average person, under those circumstances, would have been very contented to retire after 40 years of sheep and cattle herding, Moses went back into Egypt as a leader in the project of slave abolishment.

As you remember, Moses then personally led those millions of Hebrew people out of Egypt and across the desert to the Promised Land. Of course, he saw a few miracles like the Red Sea opening up for the Hebrew people to cross over on the dry bottom and then close again drowning the pursuing Egyptian soldiers. He also experienced a few heartaches and heartbreaks along the way.

There is no doubt that Moses accomplished what very, very few will ever come close to in this life. He has been acclaimed as one of the greatest men of all times. His life and achievements have been the source of millions of sermons and lectures and children today are still told to learn lessons from his life.

Moses represents infinitely more than just a good leader. He represents an outstanding example of a man who discovered that evasive and illusive concept you have been reading about. You have just read a short recap of his life for one purpose and one purpose only. That is, to help you grasp the significance of that concept, that basic law of life that is desperately needed if you are going to be an active and enthusiastic member of the 19%.

Do not misunderstand. This does not mean that you are not enjoying the finest things of life in the way of success, happiness, and security just because you are not leading an entire nation. Neither does it mean that when people discover these basic laws of life and use them to their utmost, they will only be involved in religious endeavors.

What is so vital in all this is that the 81% do not come to an understanding of this basic law and act on it like Moses.

In other words, the 19% found it and got an exciting comprehension of it. Then, they ran with it for all it is worth.

If you are going to have the happier, healthier, and more secure life then you must comprehend this basic law and all the thrilling ramifications of it. Once you do and *then* follow through, there is no limit to what you can do and enjoy.

For fear that, because this law is so simple, and the word that describes it is so simple, it might lose some of its fantastic potential, look first at one word of nine letters, but with unlimited significance.

The word is character. Character is described as "the combination of marks or traits belonging to an individual that distinguishes him or her from others."

There is one manuscript in existence today that has defied all the laws of modern merchandising and marketing. It has outlived all its critics in every age. It has been the source of much controversy, yet its words have never been altered or compromised. It has been, and still is, the bestselling book of all books. Some swear at it and others by it. It has been a thorn-in-the-flesh to some and a thrill-in-the-heart to others. It is, by all standards, the most unique writing ever placed together in one volume.

Before you get turned off by what you might consider a sudden switch to religion, think this through: this book, the Bible, claims that this planet earth did not come into being by some freak accident in which two meteors clashed into each other and ignited, creating a large ball of fire in space, which slowly cooled down and attracted dust and foreign particles and debris from other celestial objects until it became a gigantic mass.

This Bible reveals that there is One Supreme Being who meticulously created the earth and all that is in it. It further teaches that this same Supreme Being not only exists, but is the highest form of existence.

It teaches that this Supreme Being is the quintessence of love and that not only did He create man, but loves him. It states in a very sensible way that He created the earth and its inhabitants through His love so that they would enjoy life at its best.

Now, do not let this soar over your head.

The Bible reveals one vital fact that you must know if you are going to understand these laws and see them work for you. That is, the Creator of mankind also endowed that same creature with certain, specific powers. If that is a little heavy, try this: God gives every single human being talents, powers, and abilities.

This is so crucial to learning why only a few go beyond mediocre existence that you need to let it sink into your mind, going all the way down into the subconscious and fixing itself in an unmovable position.

What all this means is very simple. You are endowed with certain inalienable powers that are yours and yours alone. They are as much a part of you as your eyes, nose, and mouth. Just as you were given the breath of life whereby you live, you were given abilities to excel in specific endeavors. In the same manner as you had a natural inner-urge and desire that could only be satisfied by the warmth and nourishing milk of your mother's breasts or something very, very close to it, you also have that same natural inner-urge to exceed in a certain, specific endeavor.

The very reason why the majority of creatures on this planet earth never, ever come to the realization of their capabilities and potentials is that they have never, ever come to the thrilling understanding and exciting acceptance of this dynamic fact. They never, ever grasp the sensational fact that they have hidden inner-powers placed as an intricate part of their lives by their Creator!

This is the very reason why there is so much frustration, defeat and mediocrity today. Only a microscopically small percentage of 20th century human beings ever come to the knowledge that they do have these special gifts and talents—much less ever seek to find out what they are and develop them to their highest potential.

When only a very, very few—the nineteen percent—ever come to this awareness and then go on to use these gifts, it stands to reason that the rest—the eighty-one percent—are left with little more than survival and existence.

Don't get me wrong. There can be, and usually are, periods of enjoyment along the way for the majority, but never that lasting satisfaction and genuine fulfillment of being all a person can be.

Like the much-repeated story of the peasant lady enduring the cold and dampness of the ship's cargo area as it sailed closer and closer to America. She had worked hard and long, saving every penny she could from doing other people's washing and ironing, so she could buy

passage to the free land. Now she was aboard.
She knew that once she arrived her life would
take on a new dimension.

As you probably know, one of the crewmen
found her. When he asked her what she was
doing down there, she pleaded to stay, insisting
that she was doing no harm.

The crewman asked for her ticket and then
said, "Lady, you don't belong down here trying
to exist on a few crackers. Your ticket entitles
you to be eating in the main dining room with
all the other paid passengers!"

Your entrance into this world entitled you,
by the price paid by your Creator, to not only
use, but to enjoy to the fullest, your rightful,
individual talents. They are yours! No one else
can lay claim to them. They belong to you and
you only!

Before you can embark on the greatest and
most exciting adventure you ever dreamed of—
your fulfillment and enjoyment of successful
life and endeavors—you must fully and completely believe and accept wholeheartedly, the
undeniable fact that you most definitely have
special and unique powers and that these powers are ready and waiting for you to take them
to their limit.

The famous German composer, Ludwig von
Beethoven, died in 1827 at the age of 57. To
the small group of friends and relatives near
his death bed on that fateful day he gave his
last six words, They were, "Applaud friends,
the comedy is over."

To live 57, 157 or 1,057 years without discovering and utilizing to their fullest your God-
given gifts, abilities, talents, or powers would

be to make your life more of a tragedy than a comedy.

Once you begin to fully comprehend and accept the fact that you received certain specific and individual abilities that are distinctly yours when you came into this world and realize also that no one can take them from you, you are on your way to achieving more than you ever dreamed possible.

Furthermore, it is thrilling, and absolutely vital, to know that no one can deny you this God-given endowment. They are yours even though tyrants could prevent you from using them. But in this free society, you can use them to their maximum.

Since your Creator gave you gifts, He naturally wants you to make the best use of them. That's reasonable, isn't it?

Then, it is also reasonable that since He wants you to make the best use of them, He is going to have to, somehow, make you understand what those powers are.

Since He has given you these powers, it makes even more sense that you would want to have God give you a little of His superior intelligence and judgment of guiding, instructing and planning in conjunction with those gifts. Consider this promise of God, "I will instruct thee and teach thee in the way which thou shalt go . . ."

It is vital for you to understand something about what you just read. Too many people have fallen far short of their enjoyment in life because they came to the false and deadening conclusion that this business of the Creator's communicating with His creatures is only in the realm of religious activities.

God has not endowed human beings with powers, talents, gifts and abilities so that everyone of them can become missionaries and go to far off jungles and work with half-naked savages.

Just as God established fixed laws like that of gravity for your safety and overall benefit, He has also entrusted man with fixed laws of character development, fulfillment in life, and overall satisfaction, success, and security. God gives to mankind, His creatures, these powers to think positively, enthusiastically, constructively, happily, and successfully.

CHAPTER FIVE
EVERYONE HAS ONE

Today there are almost as many diseases as there are doctors. Many of them are crippling and many fatal. Yet, one of the most insidious infections known to modern man is not even classed as a malady. Despite the fact that it can readily be recognized as more than a national epidemic, afflicting the majority, no one has yet placed it in the contagious catagory. It is most definitely communicable.

This debilitation can be summed up in two words. They are "worry" and "doubt." And these two enfeebling words are the greatest hinderances to your being able to wholeheartedly accept your God-given talents, powers, gifts, and abilities. Carried to their full powers, they can wreck any and all lives. It can prevent even the most intelligent and sincere person from discovering his or her tremendous potentials as well as their utilization.

Charles Mayo, the world famous surgeon, and founder of the massive clinic in Rochester, Minnesota named after him, once said, "Worry affects the circulation, the heart, the glands, the whole nervous system. I have never known a man who died from overwork, but many who died from doubt."

Doubt and worry bring about just the opposite of God's intended purposes for you. They actually cause you to think more about the things you do not want to happen than what you do want to happen in your life.

Worry and doubt create a mental block. This video barrier to accepting and acting on these sensational concepts becomes a physical misconception. That is, your thoughts become focused on false concepts about yourself. In other words, worry and doubt bring about incorrect evaluations about the total person.

The proof is seen in the fact that most people consider themselves unattractive. In addition, the "born on the wrong side of the tracks" stigma becomes a resistance to God-given powers. Another prominent weight that hangs heavily on many individuals' shoulders is what they consider to be shyness and reservedness, or a tendency to be uneasy and uncomfortable among other people.

Through these, and many other, misconceptions, the vast majority, the eighty-one percent, do not think that they have the kind of aggressive personality, background, appearance, or drive they feel necessary to success.

All these barriers make up what is known as inferiority complexes. This may come as a shocker, but every normal human being that is a part of modern, active society has an inferiority complex! That is right. From Miss America to the man whose body ripples with muscles as he reaches out for the body building crown, every single person alive has an inferiority complex. The difference in the happy, successful and secure person is that he or she has come to grips with this fact and has learned how to master it and make it work for him instead of against him.

Abraham Lincoln was, by far, not the most handsome or graceful man who ever attempted to be a lawyer and politician. By modern standards, he was too tall, too thin, too awkward, and too much aware of it to ever make anything out of his life. After many real lessons in the college of hard knocks, he realized that success isn't dependent on physical attributes. He also learned that many men who were making their mark in the world were even less handsome, and many of them did not have too many of those other elements he felt were vital; so, he used all he had for all it was worth.

As to not being born with a financial advantage or social status, Ole Honest Abe, himself, said, "It's not where you came from that matters, but where you are going."

The majority in the eighty-one percent bracket are not there because they have an inferiority complex, but because they have not learned how to handle it. A certain young man did not participate in many secondary school games and activities because his overprotective mother had said many times, "You can't run and play much because you have asthma and will get really sick." So, he did not get active in high school and college sports because of his "handicap." When he enlisted in the military service to avoid the draft, he was forced to do many things he never felt he was capable of doing. He even discovered, to his sheer delight, that he could actually do some things better than a number of the other guys in his outfit. Then, his inferiority complex turned into a temporary resentment towards his mother and kept him back for a long time. Today, after coming to the knowledge that every other person has a complex dealing with it, he is the president of his own company.

When you realize that every person, male or female, that you will meet or talk with in the future has his or her own inferiority complex, you will find that it gives you more self-confidence. You can be listening to him [or her] and thinking in a wholesome way, "He [or she] has an inferiority complex just like everyone else. He [or she] is insecure, too. I'm just as good and capable as he [or she] is." It literally lifts you up to the place where you no longer have to look up, but you can now see everyone else "eye to eye."

Now you can understand that obnoxious man who constantly jokes and can come up with the latest humorous story as he slaps you on the back. He is trying to deal [in his own way] with his complex. He is trying to present a happy, cheerful, and free portrayal of what he feels is the acceptable and likeable person. He is trying to cover over his definite unhappiness and insecurity.

By the same token, that man or woman who sits in the corner, or the ones who must have every word dragged out of their mouths in strained conversations, are trying to deal with their own complexes—though in the opposite way—from the rash, motor-mouthed joker's method. These people are afraid to speak for fear they will say the wrong thing. They are afraid to act and make a mistake. They are terrified of not being accepted.

Regardless of which extreme people go to in their attempts to be normal and well-liked, the shyness or brashness is a neon sign flashing out their complexes.

Do not misunderstand this. It is not a matter of "misery loves company," but an acknowledgment that can only help you. Understanding that everyone else has a problem or problems, and that you are not an isolated, pathetic case, can only give you more courage. So what, if you may not win a Mr. or Miss America title, you can walk away with the top prize, the crown, the victor's cup in the most important contest of all—the triumph of your own personal integrity, pride and self-confidence.

Inferiority complexes, recognized as such and properly dealt with, can no longer keep any sincere man or woman down as a defeated person. Regardless of age, once you face the proven fact that all the people you will rub elbows with in mad pursuit for meaning and fulfillment in life have hang-ups and handicaps and are desperately trying to handle them, your own private and personal skeletons in the closet can no longer keep you back.

A few years ago, a billboard advertisement appeared everywhere. It pictured a small boy looking bravely right into the eyes of the local bully. Gone from the smaller boy's face was the fear the bully was able to engender in practically all of the other young boys. There was even a look of confidence unseen on any others his age and size. What made the difference in the small lad's attitude this time? His left arm was extended upward where his hand held tightly the hand of his own big brother.

And this is exactly what you need. You need to be able to reach up and grasp the hand of your Creator, and have Him lead you upwards towards the realization of your full potentials!

Let's re-think things for a moment or two.

God created man in His image.

He made man to be happy and healthy.

The Lord said, "I am come that they might have life, and have it more abundantly."

In order for man to have that exciting and rewarding, complete life, He "built-in" talents, powers and gifts.

If any man is to realize and use those powers, then God must show them to man. Man must have a heaven-sent wisdom.

CHAPTER SIX

THE BREAKTHROUGH

The residents of Central Florida are adjusted to the annual winter increase in tourists and traffic. With Disney World, Epcot, Sea World, Circus World, Busch Gardens, and Cypress Gardens attracting millions each year, they become accustomed to the nation's looking over the area. But one day the nation focused its attention not to these attractions, but on the tiny town of Starke. And for a different and awesome reason.

One news reporter described the horrible scene to his radio listeners this way, "At 10:10 A.M. his fingers turned white as his hands gripped the chair tightly. At 10:12 A.M. white smoke came out from under his face mask, and his body slumped forward in the electric chair. At 10:16 the doctors pronounced him officially dead. He had cried a couple of times before he spoke his last words. They were, "I hold malice toward none. May God bless you all."

When 36 year old Robert Sullivan became the ninth person to be executed after the reinstatement of the death penalty, these words became even more meaningful to this book,

"Of all sad words of tongue and pen, the saddest are these, 'it might have been.' "

What might have been if Robert Sullivan had listened to the RIGHT FORCE in this all-out battle for human lives? It is quite obvious that he had the wrong instructor.

What will happen to you if you, by some slight possibility, listen to the wrong instructor?

Before you answer that question, or even throw it out because you think it is impossible for you to be guided by any evil supernatural power in any way, answer this question:

How do these two powers, forces, characters actually influence human beings?

Surely, there is a method whereby God communicates ideas to His creatures. And surely, there is a viable way in which He can impress men and women. The One who created this world without the use of any pre-existing matter whatsoever could easily devise a program of interplanetary communication. And He did!

Each fall and early winter, thousands of residents of the northern section of the United States start heading out for Florida in motor homes, vans, cars, and trucks with travel trailers tagging along behind. They plan their trips each year, with specific overnight stops in certain cities enroute. Despite the fact that many have made the trip for years, the trusty road map is a vital part of their escape from the cold and snow.

The cars are tuned up, the oil changed, the tires properly aired, and a hundred and one things done even months before their departure for warmer weather and brighter skies. A lot of planning precedes their trips.

Many simply make round trips by commercial airlines. They prefer to sit back in a comfortable lounge-type chair and be lifted up into the skies to be speeded to their destination in a matter of a few hours. All the time the refreshments are being served and the magazines are being read while people sleep, the pilot, co-pilot, and navigator are busy at work reading the hundreds of complicated dials, checking maps and communicating with control towers hundreds of miles away.

Modern travel is genuinely a much easier task than that of just a half century ago. But look at another "snow-bird" and the unusual trip he makes.

His trip is at least 2,000 miles.

It is almost non-stop.

And, of course, it is by air.

He leaves Alaska in the fall and makes his first refueling stop in Hawaii after flying across the Pacific Ocean.

Then, he is in the air for the remainder of his trip to Australia.

He has no maps and no radio communications with control towers.

He flies at an altitude of from 3,000 to 21,000 feet.

And he is only about 10 to 11 inches long!

The American Golden Plover makes his spectacular flight through his built-in power called instinct. You recognize this, along with many other amazing acts of birds and animals, as a God-given impulse that incites them to actions that are essential to their existence, preservation, and development.

Even more exciting is the complex system set up for human beings.

"Mens agitat molem."

You may have heard those three specific words quoted many times, but chances are good that you do not know who originated them. Have you ever heard of the Roman poet who lived in the century just before Christ who was named simply Virgil? Historians attribute these words to him.

Right now you may be thinking, "often quoted? Man, I never heard those words before in my life, much less know what they mean."

But the English version you do know. "Mind moves matter." Through the years, some have changed them to become "Mind over matter."

Okay, if mind moves matter, what moves the mind?

Domenico Cotugno had wondered about this, too. And he began the world's rush to the discovery on October 2, 1784.

The Naples professor of anatomy was dissecting a live mouse for a demonstration. He held the wiggling specimen upside down by grasping the skin of its back between his thumb and two fingers. He also clasped the tail between the last two fingers of the same hand.

"I had hardly cut through the animal's stomach skin," he wrote, "when the mouse vibrated his tail between my fingers, and was so violently agitated against my third finger, that to my great astonishment, I felt a shock through my left arm as far as to my neck, attended with an internal tremor, a painful sensation in my arm muscles, and with such giddiness of the head, being afraid, I dropped the mouse.

The stupor of my arm lasted upwards to a quarter of an hour.... I had no idea such an animal was electrical; but in this I had the positive proof of experience."

His experience caught the attention of leading scientists. The phenomenon of "animal electricity" led to the investigation of the nervous system and the amazing connection of the brain to the nervous system.

It was later discovered that the nervous system could be compared to the high speed, message-flashing telegraph system.

This led to ESB, electrical stimulation of the brain, and all the eye-opening discoveries that followed. Scientists and physicians today are almost daily seeing fantastic revelations of the brain and its complex capabilities. But the implanting of electrodes into the brain has fascinated and challenged the greatest of scientific minds. And it is the implantation of electrodes to manipulate actions and thoughts that has laid the ground work for the acceptance of this very concept you are to soon discover.

What has boggled minds for years became so clear and conceivable that it is now considered by many to be elementary.

This life-altering concept can be wrapped up in just ten words:

God impresses human beings through electrical impulses to the brain!

Mind moves matter, but, the concept says, electrical impulses move the brain.

Naturally, even though our scientific investigations have been rapid and very advanced, the statement that "God impresses human

beings through electrical impulses to the brain"
encompasses an even more intricate program.

The most imaginative minds have found it
difficult to grasp.

Nevertheless, enough has been discovered to
indicate that this is more than a concept, much
more than a theory.

Right here, it might be well to stop and ask
you a few questions.

You are reading this book in a search for
success and fulfillment in life. You have been
thinking about the type of real career, or life
after a career, that you should have. In the
middle of this book about self-motivation based
on talents, gifts, and powers that are distinctly
yours, you find yourself confronted with the
idea of God's showing you what particular skills
He gave you at birth. This subject might be
disturbing to some people.

"Do you feel just a little uncomfortable with
this?"

If you have hesitations because of the religious connotation this concept has suddenly
drawn you into, and if you are not accustomed
to this subject, then please consider something
that happened recently in Green Belt, Maryland,
in conjunction with some unusual space program researches.

Scientists in the space program there were
trying to make some very unusual calculations.
That is, they were checking the position of the
sun, moon, and planets in space to determine
where they would be 100, or 1,000 years from
now. They must lay out the orbits in terms of
the life of the satellite, and where the planets

will be at that same time so the whole thing will not bog down.

The scientists have to determine exactly where the various planets will be in outerspace so that when a satellite is sent up, it will not bump into something later on in its orbits.

In the process of determination, they sent the computer measurement back and forth over the centuries, and, all of a sudden, the computer came to a halt!

When the computer stopped and sent up a red signal, it was immediately known that something was wrong either with the information being fed into it, or with the results as compared with the standards. The service department was called in to check it out. The computer was perfect in every way, so it was not the machine.

The information that had been fed into the computer was correct. Then came the startling discovery.

They found that there is a day missing in space in elapsed time!

The scientists were baffled. The question that most made them tear out their hair was, "How could there be a day missing in space in elapsed time?"

One man on the team who attended church regularly said, "You know, one time our minister talked about the sun standing still."

This brought an immediate roar of laughter from the frustrated workmen. No one believed it was possible. But after a while, someone said, "Show us where the Bible says that."

Even though it was embarassing and difficult, he searched his Bible until he found what sounded like a ridiculous statement for anyone with any common sense at all to accept. It was in the book of Joshua. Joshua was surrounded by an enemy force. As the commander-in-chief, he was very concerned for the safety of his men, as well as for himself. He just knew that if darkness came, the enemy would overpower them. So, according to the Bible, Joshua asked God to make the sun stand still. It is recorded in Joshua, chapter ten and verses eight through thirteen.

A stillness came over the workroom as these words were read: "The sun stood still, and the moon stayed . . . and hasted not to go down about a whole day . . ."

The spacemen actually exclaimed, "There's the missing day!"

They checked the computers going back into the time that incident was written and found that it was close, but not close enough!

The elapsed time that was missing back in Joshua's day was twenty-three hours and twenty minutes. 23 hours and 20 minutes do not make a whole day!

Reading the account again they noticed that it said, "about a whole day." Those words were very, very crucial. The scientists had a problem.

If they could not account for forty minutes, they would still be in trouble 1,000 years from now. 40 minutes multiplied many times over in orbits could create havoc.

Then the religious man remembered something about the sun's going BACKWARDS. This time his fellow-scientists declared he was mad. With a great deal of difficulty, he found the sensational story in the book of Second Kings

where King Hezekiah, on his deathbed, asked
for a sign that he was not going to die. Isaiah
the prophet asked if he would like for the sun
to go ahead ten degrees. The King asked for an
even more impossible sign. He asked that the
sun go BACKWARDS ten degrees. When they
went out and stood before the sundial, the
shadow actually turned backward ten degrees
right before their eyes!

Ten degrees is exactly 40 minutes!

When the scientists added the 40 minutes in
Second Kings to the 23 hours and 20 minutes
in Joshua, they had their missing 24 hours
and they put that in the logbook as the missing day in the universe.

You see, archeologists have been able to prove
that the historical events in the Bible are accu-
rate as well as factual. For instance, you read
about Moses and his successful leadership over
a couple of million Hebrews as they moved
from slavery in Egypt to their new free land. It
has been confirmed that Thutmose I was the
ruler and the famous Hatshepsut was his
daughter, and the one who discovered Moses in
his little nautical-craddle.

In other words, day after day, in many different ways, more and more people are coming
to the realization that the Bible is a reliable,
factual, communication from Creator to creature.

Look at these next twenty-three words from
the Bible, that book of written communication
from the Creator to His creatures. "If any of
you lack wisdom, let him ask of God, that
giveth to all men liberally, and it shall be
given him [James 1:5]. Three words were under-
lined in that sensational promise. The reason

is obvious. The promise is not made to certain selected individuals, but to "any." The revealing of wisdom [to understand and use talents] is not limited to a few, but to "all!" And this is all guaranteed! "And it *shall* be given."

The American lawyer William Herndon wrote a great deal about another lawyer, Abraham Lincoln. Herndon said of Lincoln, "He firmly believed in an overruling Providence, Maker, God, and the great moral of Him written in the human heart." That is why Abraham Lincoln is said to have written, "I am satisfied that when the Almighty wants me to do, or not to do any particular thing, He finds a way of letting me know."

You CAN know it. One thing Lincoln did not state was how to go about making absolutely positive that impressions are from God. You just read how. You ASK!

It may seem strange, but there are people who are actually terrified of that three-lettered word, "ask." Terrified, that is, of asking God. Yet, why should they be?

When your Ford station wagon starts to sound like a Singer Sewing machine, and you are not too mechanically inclined, do you go to the corner McDonald's hamburger stand and ask the attendant at the drive-in what she thinks might be the problem?

When the water in your shower starts turning cold, although you have the hot water faucet on, and you have checked the electrical panel box, and found that electricity is definitely going to the water heater, do you get on the phone, after drying off, of course, and call the salesman at Radio Shack?

When your office typewriter starts printing !,@,#,$,%, instead of 1,2,3,4,5 and you are not pressing down the Shift button that capitalizes the letters and gives you symbols above the number keys, do you look in the telephone directory to get assistance from a health food store?

No, in order for you to get help and instruction for particular needs, you ask the expert in that field.

And this is exactly what you are to do now. You have a need. You want wisdom to know what you are to do with your young, middle-aged, or elderly life. So, you ask the One who is The Expert.

Right now, it might be well to erase a big misconception about this business of asking the Creator. Too many times, there is the damning vision that has been created by too many "professional" clergymen. You can picture them right now, can't you, with their long flowing black robes as they ascend up into a high and lofty pulpit, way above the pews in their majestic, stained-windowed buildings. With an air of refined and polished purity, they step forward to make their sublime supplications to their Maker for His subjects congregated within the hallowed walls. The words seem to flow with a pompous perfection that could only come from much practice and rehearsal. "Oh, thou great Jehovah, seated yonder in Thy majestic throne, surrounded by Thy rainbow of love and mercy, cast Thine eyes downward to Thy humble servant and Thy waiting congregation. We beseech Thee" . . . on and on and on.

A concerned man has written, and told, this

story in contrast to that sugary and sancti-
monious, self-glorification. He pictures a young
businessman pulling his car into the drive after a hard day at work. His two children, a boy
and girl, ages 7 and 9, come running out to
meet him. As he hugs them, one says, "Oh,
thou great Father, coming home from thy special place of employment, wherein thou dost so
adequately provide for these thy two humble
children, we beseech thee, take us to yonder
drug store for a couple of ice cream cones."

There is no prescribed set of words required
to talk to your Maker. The need and desire of
your heart gives you a direct line to Him.

There are no specified places you must be in
order to communicate with your Creator. Regardless of where you are, you may have an
instant audience with God.

And there are no select individuals who may
have dialogues with Divinity. Since He made
YOU, He wants to help YOU.

And since He has promised to impress those
who diligently and sincerely ask Him, it would
seem feasible to consider the possibility that
He will do it for you.

Consider, now, how this might all come about.

There are two segments to this concept: First,
your Creator gave you specific powers, talents,
or gifts. Second, He will, when you truly ask,
reveal them to you.

Also, you have learned about the concept
that God speaks to human beings through electrical impulses to the brain.

How, then do all these fit together?

If you can come up with a sensible and work-
able answer to one question concerning human

behavior, or misbehavior, you will start to fit these all together. That question is long, but it is this:

"Can you determine why otherwise very smart and sensible men and women will spend the same amount of money it would take to buy a brand new Cadillac with all the extra optional equipment on it, and waste that amount on a certain act that has been clinically proven to not only shorten their lives, but to probably cause severe pain and hospitalization prior to that shortened life?"

In other words, why do people smoke?

It is far from a natural act.

It takes a lot of practice to accomplish it according to custom.

It is offensive to others who do not smoke.

It does not, despite the claims, calm the nerves, but agitate them.

So, why do people smoke?

There is only one reason why people smoke. It is called "peer pressure." Smoking to most youth indicates that the person doing it is not a "square," is "with it," and not out of touch. It is one of the most viable methods used to be accepted by the rest of the gang or friends.

Young people desperately want to be accepted by other young people.

Just as in trying to down beer and other stronger social drinks, the young person learns to smoke simply to keep from being ostracized, boycotted or snubbed by those they feel are popular or who make up the social clique.

This is why you see coughing, gagging, young people working so hard trying to become casual and cool smokers.

In order to smoke, a person has to repeat that process over and over again until the subconscious brain accepts the fact that the person wants to smoke so badly that he or she has to reverse, negate, and end many natural functions of the body. Therefore, the brain begins to reverse, negate, and end some very vital bodily functions. When this has been accomplished, addiction has set in.

Please let this sink in as it is a vital piece of understanding you must grasp and grasp fully. It has such an important function in the revelation of the Creator's will for your life that its necessity cannot be overstressed. Remember, you are looking at the concept of God speaking to you through electrical impulses to your brain. And this little illustration of the smoker's addiction will make it so very, very clear.

First, repetition changes concepts.

Repetition establishes other concepts.

And repetition really comes into play in the process of your having divine impulses to show you your powers and potentials.

Think of the amazing fact that repetition actually changes character.

When there is a repetition of certain thoughts, certain actions follow. The repetition of those specific actions create a habit. And the repetition of those habits creates an intricate part of your character.

Look at it another way. When your mind dwells on certain thoughts, you will eventually act on those thoughts. When you do that act over and over again many times, that act becomes an active habit. Repeating that habit many times will make that habit a "natural" part of your makeup; and therefore will play an important and leading part in the development of what you actually turn out to be. In other words, it establishes your character.

If you were to go to a large book store and buy every book on the subject of self-help, especially in the field of successful business, sales, and motivation, you would find the same basic string of this same concept weaving in and out of each and every book.

If you attended every self-help seminar, clinic, or program that will be conducted this next year, there would be a difference in the presentations, as well as in the personalities of the leaders and speakers, but you would see a central theme emphasized over and over again.

These highly paid motivation trainers go through many varied exercises to try to achieve the same purpose. That is, to get the attendants and participants to "see" their goals. Some instruct participants to spend time in writing out what they feel is their most prominent priority . . . to actually spell out their number one goal in life, even though no one else will see it. Many have these sincere people put their most cherished desire in writing.

For example, one or two of the most successful positive-thinking teachers have their audience or class sit at tables where they can place their heads face down on them, close their eyes and diligently try to picture that goal, priority, or tremendous desire. This process is not rushed in the least, so as to give the students time to try and clearly see that image.

Regardless of whether it is no more than owning and driving the biggest and most expensive car, they persuasively appeal to that person to see himself or herself in the driver's seat, gently and effortlessly moving it along the countryside.

If one's goal is to be able to provide a college education for the son, then that person is urged to picture him standing in cap and gown in front of a large audience as the president of the college hands him the ribbon-wrapped diploma.

If a goal turns out to be a home for a student, then the one who wants it is to see himself or herself out on the green carpet lawn in front of the home, looking back at its massive colonial columns holding up the ornate front porch of the two story brick work of art.

Another person might be gently instructed to see the business he would like to own and operate really flourishing as customers walk in and out, and the cash register ringing with a rewarding rhythm.

If being president of the company for which one works is that burning desire, then that person is to picture the huge office with the rich, thick carpet, the plush drapes, the window view of the factory behind and below, and that person sitting in the distinctive chair behind the mahogany desk.

Many instructors will carry this even further to have the students then draw that picture of themselves enjoying the happy outcome, the fulfillment of that dream.

And with many of these quality lecturers, the process continues with the student's taking that picture and making several copies. The copies are to be placed in strategic places where he or she can see them several times each day, particularly when awakening in the morning. By looking at that picture three, four, or five times a day, and thinking of it's one day becoming a thrilling reality, the idea becomes indelibly engraved in the most prominent and active part of the subconscious mind.

By constantly looking at, and thinking about that happy and enjoyable, fulfilled goal, the subconscious mind becomes fixated, and the person becomes obsessed with making it happen.

In addition, the subconscious slowly, but insidiously, starts bringing to the conscious mind the ways and means by which that person can make it happen.

This is a fixed law which cannot be denied.

Even though you considered this illustration before, it is a perfect example of this fixed and undeniable law. Remember "The Five Day Plan To Stop Smoking?" The leaders of this highly successful program [which does actually last only five days] stress over and over again the addiction. And to help the brain help the individual's struggle in overcoming the habit, the participant is given an exercise.

This exercise is the repetition of five choice words when the urge to smoke is great. They are to say, I choose not to smoke." That is all, but those five words set in motion the powers to break the habit. Whenever a person who is trying to stop smoking is offered a cigarette, they reply, "No thank you, I choose not to smoke."

The constant repetition of the words "I choose not to smoke" finally becomes fixed in the subconscious mind to where a desire to smoke is no longer alive. The person becomes victorious.

So, you can see that this amazing psychological fact is very simple. By putting a sought-after goal, dream or desire in a prominent place in the subconscious mind and keeping it before the mind constantly, the subconscious finally accepts it as an order, and consequently starts to carry out the order.

When anyone sincerely follows the sound psychological self-help programs for a certain period of time, and does it with all his or her heart, a certain type of success is almost surely guaranteed.

However, there is just one fallacy in all these superior programs. Not that they do not work. Contrarily, they work amazingly well. But there is one problem even in the clinics and seminars of the highest order which turn out large quantities of graduates.

Maybe you can grasp that fallacy in the following true story. And while you are trying to determine the fallacy, you might just start to grasp how you can avoid making that same mistake in your sincere desire to know your own God-given powers and potentials and to carry them to an exciting and rewarding fulfillment.

The story deals with a most unusual birthday.

CHAPTER SEVEN
THE RIGHT PLACE
AT THE . . .

John celebrated his eighteenth year of work at a Jacksonville, Florida paper mill in a bizzare manner.

With only a General Education Development high school equivalency certificate, John went to work as an apprentice millwright. By working several nights each week and an occasional weekend repairing friends' and neighbors' cars, he made ends meet. Just before going to work at the mill, he had met and married Frances. Before too long, he and Frances were proud parents of three daughters. As time crept in, John found himself in a rut. All his time and energy were spent in earning just enough to meet payments, buy groceries, and pay doctors' bills. There was an occasional treat here and there, but only occasionally.

Just after lunch in his eighteenth year at the mill, one of the foremen ran to him, yelling, "come quick. It's your Dad. He's dying!"

John's father died in his arms near the place where he had worked for years and years. That tragedy was the turning point in John's life.

John could not get his father's death off his

mind. It was not the horror of his dying in John's arms that disturbed him so much, but the fact that, just like his father, he would probably spend the rest of his life working at the very same place at the very same job and get a death-on-the-job reward for it all.

"I'm thirty-four years old," John said to himself, "And I've already worked at this paper mill more than half of my life."

Then he realized that, with the exception of a few small raises, he would go on always making just about the same wages, year after year. He felt that there had to be more to life.

So, in September of that same year, John, Frances, and the three girls moved to Lincoln, Nebraska where John enrolled in a small college. Frances worked long and hard as John burned the midnight oil trying desperately to "catch up" with the teenagers in his freshman classes.

After the first year, John took his family back to Jacksonville and began to attend the University, where the tuition and cost of living were lower. By working at the same paper mill during the summers and by Frances' continuing to work outside the home, John received sufficient funds to complete his college course.

He completed college at the age of 38.

A few months later, John enrolled in a school of optometry in Memphis, Tennessee, driving back and forth to Jacksonville on weekends until he could secure a home for all the family. Frances continued to work the additional four years until John graduated from the optometry school at 42 with his doctor's degree.

By the way, there are three things you should

know about this story. All the time that he and Frances were endeavoring to get his degree, they kept all three girls in a church-related school where the tuition was high.

Secondly, their oldest daughter had to put off going to college for one year so that her dad could graduate.

Today, Dr. John Creamer's shingle hangs outside his Central Florida office as a waving testimony to a man who discovered these concepts and put them to work.

The third thing you should know about John is that as a child he stuttered extremely. He developed a terrible inferiority complex, as you can well understand, for his stuttering continued on through the time of his entrance into college.

Today, on infrequent occasions, John might have a very slight and temporary difficulty with one or two words. But as he saw the real success of this total concept beginning to work out in his life, the handicap became less and less noticeable. He has almost a 99 percent victory.

When John's very innermost life and mind were shocked by his father's on-the-job death, he began to ask his Creator, "Is this what I am supposed to do in life?"

Day and night, on and off the job, John began to increase his petitions. "Do You have something for me to do?"

"What are my talents, dear God?" was one of his most frequent questions. And they were always followed with, "Please show me what they are."

And the repetition of this fantastic concept

began in two areas. First, John started asking his Creator to impress him with those special powers. And, second, God began impressing him!

Day after day, ever so slowly, John caught fleeting glimpses of himself as a professional man. Many times, he thought he could see himself in some type of white uniform. It was not too long before John began to consider the way out possibility of becoming a doctor. To a man with only a high school equivalency certificate, that might seem absolutely out of the question. Yet, the impressions continued to come. It may have been a contributing factor that John wore eye glasses himself, but within a few months after that terrible paper mill tragedy, John knew that he wanted to become an optometrist and help other people through that medium. His vision of becoming an optometrist is now helping him help others have better vision.

Okay, did you grasp the fallacy in these otherwise highly successful programs of self-improvement?

It was John Haywood who first said, "You can't see the forest for the trees." In today's fast-paced world, it is very, very difficult to see the forest of true success for the many trees of human definition. In other words, the majority of these fine and helpful programs are fine and helpful as far as they go. The problem is that most of them do not go far enough.

If you were to walk out to the ocean and see one of those long fishing piers with its wooden poles sticking up out of the water and a number of people holding poles over the sides with great anticipation, you might get an odd idea.

Suppose you were to look at that pier going far out into the ocean and decide that you were going to walk on it over to China! Of course, your friends and bystanders who heard you make that declaration, would question your right to be out on the streets.

You might say, "Well, I am going to go to China. Watch and see!" Then you go out about 100 feet, stop, turn back, and wave. "I'm going, see, I'm on my way." Well, you would actually be on your way, wouldn't you?

Suppose you go on to about the half way distance of the length of the pier, stop, turn around and wave again, saying, "Look, I'm making success. I'm really making success. I'm on my way." True, you are making progress.

Then, you go another 100 feet and repeat the process. You are still making progress. You are getting closer to China.

Now, what will happen when you go just one step beyond the end of the pier? Surely your trip to China will come to a sudden and very wet end. That is, of course, if you don't decide to go the rest of the way by swimming.

The pier was good and fine as far as it went. You see, the problem is that it didn't go far enough.

And try as hard as possible to not make this sound critical, these excellent self-help programs are fine . . . up to a point. And going beyond that point is exactly what you must do in order to have true and complete happiness and success. Please note carefully those three vital words, "true and complete."

Regardless of whether you are a pre-teen, teenager, in college, a young married or single man or woman, middle-aged, near retirement, or retired, this concept is definitely for you if you want to find that "true and complete happiness and success." And the most wonderful thing about it all is that you can experience them everyday.

Unlike the game of horseshoes, "close to" these most crucial and needful conditions in life is not enough.

Robert Sullivan, who was executed in that Starke, Florida electric chair operated on a different formula from Dr. Creamer, the optometrist. And these two distinct formulas make the tremendous difference in those who are in the eighty-one per cent and those in the nineteen percent. They make the difference in one's not finding "true and complete happiness and success," and those who do.

The formula is simply this: "Being at the right place at the right time, doing the right thing with the right attitude about the right things."

Now, changing any one of these five segments in the formula will blow the whole thing.

For example, "Being in the WRONG PLACE at the right time," or "being at the right place at the WRONG TIME," or "being at the right place at the right time, DOING THE WRONG THING," or "being at the right place at the right time, doing the right things with the WRONG ATTITUDE, will of course, bring about the WRONG things."

So, you see, "close" just isn't good enough.

Now, what all this means is simply what

good does it do for a person to attend the most popular speaker's seminar on success if that person, sincere and honest as he or she may be, gets just "close" to showing his attendants "true and complete happiness?"

Two men were taking a short pickup trip to take a riding lawnmower to the dealer for correction of some manufacturing malfunction. The driver was in his early seventies and retired. The other man was in his early fifties and president of his small company. The retired man said something that really disturbed the other man. They were discussing the fact that time seems to slip up on a person and before he can even realize it, he is old. The retired man sighed, and said, "Well, I just wish that during those fast-fleeting years, I could have been a success."

The man in the passenger's side of the pickup looked into his friend's eyes, and said, "Why do you feel that you have not made a success in your life? Aren't you happy?"

"Well," the senior citizen hesitatingly replied, "I guess you can say I'm happy. But I just feel like I've never really accomplished anything."

It was quite strange for the younger man to listen to the older one as he went on elaborating on what he might have done. Strange, because the pickup was relatively new and paid for. The senior citizen owned a home in the northern section of the country, and had purchased [with cash] five acres of Florida land within the previous one year. This senior citizen had recently built a nice concrete block garage on that property, doing an extremely neat and admirable job of laying the blocks himself. He was going to go back to his home and sell it. Then, he was planning to return to that property and place a nice double-wide mobile home with many fine conveniences in it near that new large garage.

The passenger was still thinking about the fact that this man had a very fine Christian wife who had been extremely supportive of him in their over fifty years of marriage. Two lovely girls with high standards had graced their home. A very industrious and personable son, who also had high morals, was given them.

As the truck neared the little town where the mower dealer was located, the passenger continued his evaluation of his friend. He had an appealing smile, a good sense of humor, a sharp mind, exceptionally fine health, and. . . .

"Yeah, but you don't understand," his friend said as he broke into his train of thought, "I just haven't succeeded in anything."

"Well, tell me," the younger man said, "exactly what success is."

After a long pause, a few unfinished sentences were uttered that did not define success. The mower shop appeared ahead of them and the conversation was never finished.

There is absolutely no way humanly possible for a person to perfectly carry out the formula of "being at the right place at the right time, doing the right thing with the right attitude about the right things" UNTIL he or she has the Creator reveal those special powers, talents, gifts and potentials, and then pursue the fulfillment of them with all his or her heart!

You can actually carry out this formula, and carry it to an exciting fulfillment that you never dreamed was possible. Like Confucius said, "A trip of a thousand miles begins with the first step."

Examine, now, that first step.

CHAPTER EIGHT

IMPRESSIONS

The barbers and hairstylists of America were having a national convention a few years back in New York City. The board of directors had a burden. It was to try to elevate their role in the eyes of the people. Being proud of their profession, they wanted to lift it higher in esteem. They hired a young publicity agent who immediately went to work.

He went into a certain section of New York where the defeated and derelicts congregate and found another young man who, beneath an unclean face, long, unkept hair, and a dirty beard, was apparently nice looking. He made him a proposal to earn a certain amount of money by doing a few simple things and the man agreed.

The agent took him, just as he had been found to a leading photographer and had his picture taken.

Then, he made arrangements for him to have a steam bath, hair styling, and a shave.

Back then to the photographer for the second series of photos.

A famous men's clothing store manager

helped select a complete outfit for the already improved subject. After dressing him in these smart professional clothes, the third series of photographs were taken.

There were three specific photos selected to be blown up into lifesize proportions, and taken to the hotel in which the convention was to be held. When these professional barbers arrived, they were greeted by a most unusual and attention-grabbing sign. There were the three distinct lifesize photos of, first, the man as he had been when the agent met him. Second, after he had been professionally groomed. And, third, with his new shoes, socks, shirt, tie and immaculate suit.

Above these huge photos was an even larger sign which read, "This Is What The Barbers And Hairstylists Of America Can Do For A Man."

The transformation was tremendous. Picture number one did not look anything like picture number three. Everyone who walked into that lobby paused and looked at the sensational change. Even the press was so impressed that the story and pictures went practically nation-wide.

The young man was hired to also stay there for the entire week's meeting. He had been instructed to walk around in conspicious places so that he could talk with anyone and every-one who approached him.

During his stay there as a living public rela-tions story, one of the assistant managers of the hotel talked with him several times and decided to help him. So, a mutual agreement was made that on the first Monday morning after the close of the convention, they would meet back in the assistant manager's office, sharply at 10:00.

Over the weekend, the hotel executive contacted several of his business friends and convinced one of them to agree to give this young man an opportunity to begin working in a job with a great deal of advancement opportunity.

Eagerly the young hotel assistant manager awaited the other young man's Monday morning arrival. Nine o'clock came, but the young man did not arrive. He had not arrived by ten, nor eleven, nor twelve noon. Not wanting to miss him, the assistant manager had his lunch brought into his office. All day long, he hoped and prayed that he would show up. But, to his deep disappointment, there was no meeting of the two.

Several months went by and the assistant manager was in the basement looking for something when he saw those huge photos leaning up against a wall. He immediately disbanded his project, picked up one of the photos, and went over to the area where the agent had found the young man. Holding up the picture, he asked person after person after person if they knew where he was. No one knew him. In the middle of the long and frustrating afternoon, it dawned on him that he was carrying picture number three, the one of the transformed man!

He rushed back to the hotel and made the switch. Armed with the first picture, he located him in less than an hour. Sure enough, his tie was gone, his coat was badly soiled, and his pants were torn and filthy. His hair was

long again and his beard was making an unhealthy growth. He smelled like liquor and
looked like a tramp.

The barbers and hairstylists can do outstanding jobs of making real transformation in a
person's appearance. They do wonders for individuals on the outside. The only problem is
that they cannot do any transformation on the
inside!

What that young man needed we all need
. . . inner resources.

And what the eighty-one percent need in
order to attain "true and complete happiness
and success"; to be able to "be at the right
place and the right time, doing the right things
with the right attitude about the right things;"
is that real inner resource obtained through
asking, receiving, and utilizing their Creator's
given talents.

It might be well to recognize something very
important at this juncture. That is, the Bible
makes it plain that there is not much merit, if
any, in a person's repeating written or memorized prayers. In the book of Matthew they are
referred to as "vain repetitions as the heathen
do." Regardless of the sincerity of the person,
the requests seem to be of no effect. It is not
the words, but the repetition of a heart's desire
that is all important.

There is another dynamic paradox about this
tremendous concept that is truly stranger than
fiction. It deals with the repetition aspect in
learning your special potentials.

In all probability, when you first ask your
Creator to impress you in such a way that you
will realize what powers He has given you, the

sky will not immediately turn pitch black, and a bright flash of lightning spell out the words in flaming letters. Most likely, you will not wake up in the middle of the night to find a white-robed and majestic personage standing at the foot of your bed to elaborate on those talents. And there is a good possibility you will not have the life-altering experience of hearing the most majestic and melodious voice booming down a complete description of your gifts.

In other words, the first time you ask, you may experience absolutely nothing, except a warm feeling that you have done the right thing in making a petition to God. If you can understand and accept this vital truth, then you can advance. It is more than the old adage that "if at first you don't succeed, try, try again." It is simply the outworking of that paradox.

You see, the apparent [and that is all it is, apparent] lack of an answer will cause you to ask again. Only, the second time you ask, you ask in a more intensified manner. Each time you ask, your desire becomes more meaningful. And the more meaningful it becomes, the more you will ask.

See the paradox. Each time you ask, the more you become concerned. The more concerned you become, the more you will ask.

Please look at this astonishing fact. Yours will not be the only repetition taking place. True to His perfect character and love for human beings, God will, when He sees you are earnest about knowing His will for your life, start to impress you with the answers. He starts the repetition, too.

A noted poet said, "Don't expect a thousand

dollar answer to a ten cent prayer." So, as your sincere concern increases along with your genuine petitions, your life starts to make a slow and almost imperceptible, almost undetectible, change. Your thinking takes on a different perspective.

King David reached the place where he begged, "Cause me to know the way wherein I should walk; for I lift up my soul unto Thee." It sounds strange for a king to be asking God to show him what to do to have complete happiness and fulfillment in life, doesn't it? But, God "caused" him to know. And He will "cause" you to know, too.

A very obese man was once asked how he had gotten so heavy. He replied, "Ounce by ounce."

If you were to ask a number of thrilled and triumphant ones who have seen this sensational concept work for them how they reached the place where they were able to determine what God wanted them to do, they would probably answer, "impression by impression."

And these impressions will come, you can count on it, and they will continue to come as long as you continue to whole-heartedly appeal for divine wisdom.

You may be in junior high school and ask the Almighty.

As a high school senior, your petitions will be heard.

In those difficult and distressing college days, your prayers reach your Creator.

If you have just said, "I do!" to the officiating minister's question, "Do you take this man to be your lawful wedded husband?" or "Do you take this woman to be your lawful wedded wife?", your entreaty makes direct connection with your Creator.

You can surely appeal to God for direction when you are a young adult parent.

As a member of the trying middle age group, you can eagerly solicit The Supreme Being with success.

In the uncertain pre-retirement stage, you can entreat The One who can show you your future.

As a widow or widower, you can implore The Infinite One.

And because you have entered into your retirement time, you might want more than ever to ask the Ancient Of Days for advice.

Male or female, you may receive those ever-increasing electrical impulses to your brain impressing you more and more vividly with each impulse as to what God would have you do.

Sometimes, these impressions come very slowly and sometimes not quite so slowly. They came to another John in a matter of hours. Well, maybe, the final and deciding impression came within a few hours. John had been seeking the Lord for some time before the answer seemed to suddenly jell.

You have probably seen some of John's work and were not even aware of it. Remember the attractive, full-color brochures and postcards in hotels, motels and resorts describing their services or picturing their buildings? Chances are good that some of them were produced by John.

John had worked long and hard to become a professional photographer. He became a commercial one, specializing in representing the better lodging facilities. Like many who come "close" to complete happiness, John's financial success was not quite enough. Even with an attractive and very personable wife and five lovely and active daughters, something was missing. To John, life had to have a definite purpose, some way in which a man could really make a contribution to others. There just had to be more to life than the enjoyment of family, as great and challenging as that was with five growing pre-teen and teenagers. Despite the fact that he was making enough money to enjoy a few luxuries now and then, there was still that void. So, he started asking his Creator to show him what he could do about that void.

The Jamaica Queen Boat Company hired John to make a brochure of their luxury liner. They wanted John to feature the beautiful ship coming into scenic Jamaica. John flew down to that tropical paradise. He secured the time schedule from the captain before leaving home so he could try to capture the majestic view from a rented helicopter.

With a dislike for the noise that sometimes is found in some tropical hotels and motels and with parties being carried on far into the night, and guests coming in and out all the time, John stayed in one of the guest rooms of a local hospital where the administrator was a friend.

John and his doctor-administrator friend visited together for a long time the first night. Before John ended their interesting conversation and headed for his room, his friend gave him "some good news and some bad news." He

said that the small, non-profit hospital desperately needed a good public address/intercom
system. Just recently two young college students in Tennessee had heard of their need,
and had volunteered to come down and install
a system themselves. That was really good news.

The bad news was that neither they, nor the
hospital, had the funds to pay for the two round
trip tickets.

"John," the doctor said, "those two young
men need to get down here. Neither we nor
they can provide the transportation costs." Then
he leaned forward in his chair towards John,
and asked, "Do you think you could get the
boat company to give them round trip tickets
from Miami so they can do this work for us?
We will be providing much of the equipment
costs and just can't raise enough for them, too."

John said that he would try.

As he walked out of the room and down the
hall towards the private room awaiting him,
he took an even longer look at the hospital.
John had heard a great deal about the great
work this hospital was doing for the needy
Jamaican people. He knew of his friend's
sacrifices, and that night impressions began to
come just a little faster than normal.

John wished that he were a millionaire so he
could not only provide tickets for the two young
men, but could get the hospital more modern
equipment. Impressions still came all through
the night.

When John presented the situation to the
company owners, they readily agreed to provide the transportation if the young men were
willing to provide the labor.

While doing his photographical work, impressions continued to come. The electrical impulses were pounding away at his brain.

As John was flying home, rolls of pictures in his briefcase, the impressions grew more and more impressive and explicit. It was such a simple thing, asking those ship owners to help those students help the hospital, but it was so rewarding.

John soon found himself talking out loud to himself over the drone of the engines. He was voicing the impressions. "There ought to be lots of folks who'd like to do things like those two students if they knew where to go." He thought of the fact that even though theirs was a small act, through the years many, many people would find health and happiness as a result of their labors.

"Man," John continued to vocalize his thoughts, "people could take their vacation time and really make a satisfying contribution to others instead of just regular tourist trips."

As soon as he got into his home, he burst into a long and excited recitation of his impressions with his wife.

The next day, he got his wife and secretary together and shared his ideas again. He then told them of the terrific sense of well-being he had experienced in just helping get the tickets. Then he told them what he had decided during the night. They listened intently.

"I want to send out a big bunch of letters to friends and acquaintances who have planes and who fly. I want to tell them what happened to me, and then ask them if they would be inter-

ested in doing something like those two college
students did on a work-vacation."

"Also," he added, "I want to write a second
letter to hospitals, mission outposts, and churches
in Central America, the West Indies, the northern part of South America, and Mexico. Let's
ask them if there were an organization which
would provide volunteer labor, could they use
the help."

With Ida Mae, his wife, and the secretary
helping to formulate the letters, the impressions were soon taking form.

Almost immediately, John was swamped with
return letters from both groups! Countless num-
bers of aircraft owners and pilots enthusiastically responded. They wanted to have a part.

The overseas letters were not only thrilling,
but humorous. They thought that the organization was already in active existence, and asked
when could they come!

After many days of planning, many, many
long distance phone calls, and personal trips, it
all came together. The first group of excited
men, women and young people flew to Eight
Mile Rock in Freeport in the beautiful Baha-
mas to meet John and Ida Mae in December of
1969.

For two weeks, this hard working and happy
crew completed a half-built church that had
given up to the weeds and elements when its
pastor had left to further his education in the
States.

Thus began Maranatha Flights, International,
a non-profit organization of men and women
who not only donate their skills and labor,
but who also pay their own expenses to go

around the world. They build schools, hospitals, churches, and homes for those who would not otherwise be able to have them.

Today, Maranatha Flights has a membership of over 3,000!

It has the astonishing and outstanding record of completing more than 300 large projects . . . all of them done in a matter of a few weeks each.

Recently, Hurricane David took a devastating toll on the natives in the Dominican Republic. Maranatha Flights, in co-operation with an unusual and surprising endowment, restored dignity and hope. The West German Government sets aside one half of one percent of its gross national product for benevolent work around the world. Learning of this exceptional group's interest, they funded the materials cost.

If you could go to the once-desolate Dominican Republic you would see one hundred and sixty new homes standing in honor of compassionate and sacrificial human beings who, through the impressions of one man who inspired others, discovered that life is more than making a living.

Impressions.

You will understand the ten-lettered word "impression" as never before in your life, and at the same time you will never hear it spoken or read it without an amazing chain reaction taking place. Understanding the word and the sensational background of it is just the beginning.

It is absolutely vital at this point to have you do a little "brainstraining," and investigate one of the most astounding phenomenons

ever revealed to the human mind. When this
truth is correctly understood, it finally explains
what has puzzled countless millions for centuries!
Since this axiom has been so complicated by so
many false conceptions, this author spent a
great deal of time and energy trying to "bring
the cookie jar down to the lower shelf so the
shortest child in the family could reach it." In
other words, the complicated has become un-
complicated, even though it was hard doing it.
It is written in another book in greater detail,
but briefly this is the essence of what has been
one of the most misunderstood true stories in
existence.

As you have read, the Supreme Being who
created mankind cares about His creations. He
acts in their behalf. He wants them to know
happiness and success to their fullest. Yet, there
exists today such terrible things as disease,
war, pain and death.

Since the Creator is the quintessence of order,
perfection, holiness, and sinlessness, and would
not have any of His creatures experience anything but His own characteristics and happy
state of being, then there has to be something,
or someone, foreign to all, that is at work also.
And there is. It is a "someone."

This someone is an evil power, a demon, a
beguiling spirit. The Bible calls him Lucifer,
Satan or the Devil. It also teaches—now get
this—that this demon was once an angel.

In the New Testament section of the Bible,
in the book of John, there is a quotation of
Christ about this evil power. In the eighth
chapter and verse 44, Christ said, "When he
[the Devil] speaketh a lie, he speaketh of his

own; for he is a liar, and the father of it."
Christ accepted him as a literal being. To Him
Satan is no fantasy or fairytale. The entire
Bible teaches that Satan is an arch-enemy of
God and mankind. Now, since he is an archen-
emy of God and mankind, and since God is the
creator of everything, how could it be that He
would create someone who would have some
type of infinitely degenerate intelligence so as
to bring on all the havoc, disease, crime, and
injustice we see today?

Christ said something else about Satan that
might seem to complicate things even more. In
the book of Luke, the tenth chapter and verse
eighteen, He said, "I beheld Satan as lightning
fall from heaven." Then, maybe the teaching
that Satan was an angel is correct because,
apparently, he was at one time IN heaven!

According to both the Old and New Testa-
ments, heaven is the center of the universe. It
is the tangible, literal, and visible headquar-
ters of the Creator. Heaven consists of everything we cannot find much of on earth—beauty,
love, fairness, honesty, happiness, and much
more. And if Satan were in heaven, then something traumatic must have happened!

The Old Testament prophet Isaiah gave a
great deal of detail about such things as the
birth, crucifixion, and resurrection of Christ.
He also spelled out some interesting facts about
heaven. Not only did he confirm Christ's words
about Satan having been in heaven, he gave
some fascinating details about the Devil. Isaiah
actually quoted some words from Satan's own
lips. In the fourteenth chapter of his book, verses
thirteen and fourteen, Satan, standing before a

crystal clear pool of water, looked at himself
and said, "I will exalt my throne above the
stars [the angels] of God . . . I will be like the
most High." Satan had aspirations to be God!
Now, there is a reason for all this. Look at the
full background.

In Ezekial, God gives some words for the
prophet to say to a wicked king. The prophet
was to tell the king that he was very much
like the Devil himself. In Chapter twenty-eight,
verses twelve through fifteen, this is what the
Devil and the king were like: "Thus saith the
Lord God, Thou sealest up the sum, full of
wisdom, and perfect in beauty. Thou hast been
in Eden the garden of God; every precious stone
was thy covering, the sardius, topaz, and the
diamond, the beryl, the onyx, and the jasper,
the sapphire, the emerald, and the carbunckle,
and gold; the workmanship of thy tabrets and
of thy pipes [remember that term "thy pipes"]
was prepared in thee in the day that thou wast
created. Thou art the anointed cherub that
covereth; and I have set thee so; thou wast
upon the holy mountain of God; thou hast
walked up and down in the midst of the stones
of fire. Thou wast perfect in thy ways from the
day that thou wast created, till iniquity was
found in thee."

Even though these are Old English termi-
nologies, and because the King James Version
of the Bible was written that way, you can still
figure it out.

Satan WAS created by God.

Satan was one of the two angels [or cherubs]
who stood on each side of God as He was seated
on His throne. They each reached out and over

God with one of their wings and touched each other so as to make an arch or covering,

When God created Satan he was very handsome, and his actions and examples were perfect. Then sin within himself changed all that. And, strange as it may seem, Satan created that sin *within himself-by himself!*

Sin originated within the mind of one of God's highest executives. As a matter of fact, Satan was the most honored angel. He had unequaled power among all the angels. [And the Bible states that there are hundreds of millions of angels. Think of that!]

Satan was constantly in the very presence of the Creator of all beings. He was able to see the beams of brilliant beauty that surround God; and, yet, somehow, he sinned. The Bible does explain it.

Continuing with the seventeenth verse of Ezekial, chapter twenty-eight, this is added, "Thine heart was lifted up because of thy beauty; thou hast corrupted thy wisdom by reason of thy brightness." Now you can begin to see why you read that Satan wanted to be even higher than God. He thought about his talent in so many, many wide ranges of life, and felt that he could do anything. He wanted the top position. He wanted to be President of the Universe, the chairman of the board of directors of all the planets in existence.

In order to do this, God had to be out of the way. And the most spectacular and sinister schemes ever conceived in the annals of history began. He started out to impeach God!

Since every single angel in existence loved and admired Satan, he began to work on the angels through their loyalty. One by one, in a few little groups here and there, his master-mind began to make little and seemingly inno-cent insinuations that God might have ulterior, selfish motives. He slowly started portraying God as someone being driven by an egotistical need that could only be satisfied by their worship, and by submission to His every wish.

Satan's propaganda campaign was designed to make these higher forms of life see that the laws God has placed before all His creation, could, and would, apply to those in the worlds of space, but surely not to them! Since they were wiser, more beautiful, excelled in strength, and holy beings, they could not do anything that was wrong. Therefore, they did not need any laws to govern them. So, then, God must not really trust them if He subjected them to a needless and senseless code of ethics. Since He had made laws to govern them, He did not have any true confidence in them.

Satan assumed he could get the angels to believe they were being held back in their growth and development. He also felt assured that once they accepted that, they could, as a majority, repeal those laws. Once the laws of God were repealed, the next step would be to oust God!

To be sure, in the course of his cunning pro-gram of behind-the-back whisperings, he threw in just enough hints to try to make him appear as the champion of their cause.

Incredibly, Satan presented the fact that if God were no longer in control, and if he were installed in God's place, the angels would en-joy much, much more freedom and happiness.

His quiet suggestions slipped through the entire universe and every angel ear heard them.

God watched in love and patience. When His infinite wisdom recognized the time, mercy and justice stepped in.

God' true love went out to all the entire company of angels to draw them back, but many were fooled by the covetous creature's deceptive words. The majority were not. As the conflict continued in intensity, the time came when all had to make a decision. It boiled down to their choice of leaders. Either they were to keep their trust and confidence in their Creator or accept this new teaching, the new theology, and accept the charges of Lucifer against God.

It is hard to believe, but it is true that many, many of the angels in Heaven were tricked into accepting Satan's lies! Revelation states that one-third were deceived. Therefore, something had to happen.

God decided to place Satan in a position, along with his angel followers, where the entire universe of unfallen inhabitants along with the faithful angels could judge for themselves who was correct, just, loving, and merciful. It could not be a gigantic, cosmic courtroom. You see, Satan could lie and twist facts in a persuasive way. God could not. Satan could deceive, but God could not and would not. Therefore, God decided on one specific planet where He would put Lucifer and the one-third of His created angels. And, you guessed it, it was earth!

That is why mighty Paul said in First Corinthians, Chapter four, verse nine that this earth and all its residents are a "spectacle unto the world, and to angels, and to men." The word "spectacle", in its original Greek, means "theatre." That is why Shakespeare wrote that the world was a stage and all the men and women are actors.

Every day, in every way, Satan is at work. He and the vast multitudes of wicked angels are trying to portray on this universal stage, through all men, women, and young people, that he is correct in his charges against God.

Standing off stage, he laughs and rejoices every time someone accepts a temptation and falls into sin. Each and every wicked act committed by man is another opportunity for him to look up toward heaven, shake his fist at God, and shout to all onlooking beings to observe how the majority on earth are following his liberated way of life, and to see how few, if any, are following those old restrictions of God.

By the way, he doesn't have to lie. The actors are doing a fine job in living and loving Satan's way of life.

God loved Lucifer when He created him just as He loves you and me. God did not create a liar, a self-possessed demon, a devil. Lucifer made a devil out of himself. One day, Lucifer's time of probation on earth will end. He will pay for his crimes against God and mankind. One day [and many, many feel it will not be too far off or much longer], God will close the curtain and bring this horrible scene to an end. God will be seen again as the epitome, the fullness, the extreme existence of love. Never, ever, will sin rise again. There will be heaven on earth.

But . . . back at the ranch . . .

There is a maddening pursuit of the over-throw of God. A great scheme is being carried out. Although the methods of Satan are almost impossible to understand, it does teach you the vital lesson we interrupted this chapter to bring you. It does explain why you were to launch this little "brainstraining."

Just before this amazing account of the arch-enemy of your life, you read about it's being "impossible to be going in the right direction without first getting the absolute correct directions."

You see, now, don't you, how there is a possibility for a human being to be tuned into the wrong wave lengths.

CHAPTER NINE

THE SHORT CIRCUIT

David was stunned, and even frightened, when Michelle Forman [just fifteen years old] and her friend both screamed in pain and horror as he stabbed them. He was also dismayed that they bled. He had not expected those Christmas eve, 1975, stabbings to be anything but the tidy murders he had seen in the movies.

It was all going to be different at one o'clock in the morning of July 29, of that next year. This time he had a Charter Arms .44-calibre Bulldog handgun. It would be cleaner. Donna Lauria was eighteen years old and very attractive. She had worked in an emergency medical center before her body was shattered to the extent there could be no medical help.

Donna's friend was Jody Valenti, and she was a year older. She, too, [like Donna] was from the Bronx. David's 44 bullet hit her in the thigh and she was wounded.

Rosemary Keenan's father was a New York Police Department detective. Her father had warned her not to be out late at night without an escort. On Saturday night, October the 23rd, she suddenly realized that she had been talking with Carl Denaro, whom she had met in class at Queens College, maybe too long. So, at two-thirty in the morning, Carl volunteered to ride with her in her red Volkswagen so she would feel safe. Rosemary and Carl stopped and parked on 33rd Ave. near the corner of 159th street just to keep from going home. They were talking when some man in jeans and a denim jacket walked up to Carl's side, pulled out a gun, and starting shooting into the car.

Rosemary started the car and whipped out of the parking spot and raced back to the Taxcipo Grill and helped Carl into the bar. He had received a bullet in the back of the head. Rosemary was not hurt. She was eighteen and Carl just twenty.

Donna DeMasi was sixteen. She and Joanne Lomino, eighteen, went to a movie. After eating a hamburger, they caught the bus home. The bus stopped to let them off at the corner of 262nd Street and Hillside Avenue in Queens. It was 11:45 P.M. as they walked toward Joanne's home. A man walked across the street right directly towards them. Frightened, they tried in vain to make their hands, arms, and mind cooperate. Before they could get the door key out of Donna's pocket, the man pointed a gun at them and opened fire.

When an off-duty police officer who lived next door, came out, he found a girl lying on each side of the porch in the hedges. Donna had been shot from the side. The bullet entered her body where the neck meets the shoulder. She received no nervous system damage.

Joanne was not so fortunate. She became a paraplegic.

On January 30, 1977, Christine Freund, age 26, was killed in Queens.

Virginia Voskerichian died in Queens on March 8th. She was 19.

Both Valentina Suriani and Alexander Esau, ages 18 and 20, died on April 17th. Like Virginia Voskerichian, the same killer was responsible.

Judy Placido, 17, and Salvatore Lupo, 20, were both wounded in Queens on June the 26th. Same attacker.

In Brooklyn, on July 31, 1977, the killer left Stacy Moskowitz, 20, dead and Robert Violante, also 20, blinded.

A terror swept New York from July 1976 through July of 1977. It was reported that more than three hundred policemen were involved in the frantic search for the random killer.

He was, as you will recall, a mail clerk named David Berkowitz, the "Son Of Sam."

John Wayne Gacy methodically murdered more than two dozen young men and placed the corpses in his suburban Chicago basement.

Mark David Chapman stalked a certain area until he saw ex-Beatle John Lennon appear as expected. Then Chapman shot and killed him.

Although there were some differences in each case, everyone of these men was led to crimes by the same source.

Impressions.

From the brief historical outline of the origin, the beginning, of sin and Satan, you can easily recognize that Satan has more than a doctor's degree in psychology. Not only is he a mastermind of mental manipulation, but he has had nearly 6,000 years of practice. He knows full well the power of the brain. He knows all too well what modern researchers are just beginning to realize, and that is, the subconscious mind sets in motion the forces within us to bring about whatever idea is fed into it.

Having worked on this principle to the place of near perfection, he has performed phenomenal perversions with individual people. "The son of Sam," David Berkowitz, is just one example of his power in using this great concept of electrical impulses to the brain for sinister purposes. You see, behind every act of violence, stands the evil influence of a fallen angel.

Think again about the brain's being like a computer programming whatever information is fed into it. It is a fact that whatever is fed into our brain and fed into it often and long enough, will determine what action we take.

Whatever you place within the subconscious as a desire or goal, that is exactly what the subconscious begins to move towards. This is the very reason why the teachers of self-confidence courses, along with the leadership development lecturers and instructors are finding great success in this billion dollar enterprise! They have discovered this amazing phenomenon and are bringing hundreds of thousands to the place where they are experimenting with it and achieving overwhelming results.

The conductors of the tremendously successful program called THE FIVE DAY PLAN TO STOP SMOKING [referred to earlier] relate to their audiences the story of a certain witch doctor who, without the scientific knowledge of "cause and effect," made this phenomenon work to his own desired end. The case in point was a certain young native whom the witch doctor hated. He decided to get rid of him. He laborously carved a likeness of the native man in the form of a wooden doll. He placed it at the door of the native's thatched hut late one night and drew a half moon in the sand. When the man came out the next morning and discovered the doll with a stick in its heart alongside the half moon engraved in the sand, he knew he was going to die at the time of the half moon.

The amazing thing is that when that time came, the native died with no apparent cause of death whatsoever!

When that native's mind accepted the fact that he was to die at the time of the half moon, all his bodily functions were set in motion to bring about this death. They were simply shut off by the brain and he went to sleep . . . permanently!

This one incident, stunning but true, is a perfect example of how Satan has worked such a phenomenal program of keeping human beings far, far from coming even close to the realization of their God-given powers. This insidious campaign for human failure through every means possible and conceivable [and even many inconceivable] has just one goal in mind. That is to keep everyone from reaching his or her purpose in life, and thereby never knowing complete happiness. Personal happiness is a definite affront to Satan. He has charged that God's ways only lead to unhappiness and misery, which, of course, are the end results of his own ways. And each happy and successful person is a living contradiction to his claims and concepts. Therefore, it stands to reason that he does everything in his almost unlimited power to keep the majority from finding anything akin to peace, contentment and fulfillment.

In the New Testament, the mighty apostle Paul discovered this great truth and tried to get everyone to see it. He said, "For we are not fighting against people made of flesh and blood, but against persons without bodies—the evil rulers of the unseen world, those mighty satanic beings and great princes of darkness who rule this world; and against the huge number of wicked spirits of the spirit world."

The bottom line is that the battle for human lives is far greater than most people ever realized. And it is this very battle that has started to wake people up to the fact that it is vital what they allow themselves and their children to watch on television. More and more people are becoming aware of the tremendous effect outside influences make on their thinking. Some people are so concerned that they refuse, unless it is a matter of life or death, to have any type of anesthesia, except local, so as to insure that their mind could not possibly come under the control of any outside influence.

Now, in light of all these sensational facts, it just makes more sense to realize that only this concept of allowing your life to be directed in full by your Creator can bring about your total happiness and true fulfillment in life. You must have His will impressed so deeply in your mind that your actions will be programmed accordingly.

And it goes without saying that a sinless,

pure, holy, and loving Creator could not, and will not, place sinful, impure, unholy, or unloving impressions within one of His creature's mind. God never sends a bad thought to a man, woman or child!

Therefore, this same loving God will not impress anyone on this earth to do anything, go anywhere, or say anything opposite to His own perfect character. In other words, if a person has an impression which continues to embed itself deeper and deeper into his or her subconscious mind, and that impression is to steal, murder, rape, inflict bodily harm, lie, or cheat, then you can know positively that God did not do the impressing.

The Bible records some advice from the smartest king who ever lived. And in this little "homespun" statement lies one of the most tremendous psychological breakthroughs in understanding the criminal mind.

Solomon said, "Teach a child to choose the right path, and when he is older he will remain upon it." As it is well known, many very successful men and ladies will attribute their triumphs to early childhood training. The influence of the home cannot be overestimated. However, those eighteen words reveal one of the secrets of Satan's stupendous success.

You see, in analyzing the criminal's background, it is many times a complete shock to realize that he or she had many, many advantages and opportunities to make a significant contribution to society and mankind in general. As a matter of fact, some of the most brutal murderers or sadistic rapists came from fine homes with excellent atmospheres and influences. They simply do not become menaces to society overnight!

The enemy of mankind has studied man's mind all these centuries. He is a past-master in the art of brain analysis. And through his well-trained and much experienced associates, his program begins with birth. Picture the average child still in the crib. A God-given need for food creates hunger. The hunger creates emotion. The emotion creates crying. Crying brings the food in solid or liquid form.

Also picture the child, adequately fed, lying in a comfortable crib, clothes dry and fresh. Then, without any apparent reason, the child starts to cry. When there is no immediate response and the child is not picked up and held, rocked or rubbed, the cry sound becomes a scream. The scream continues until the desired attention is given.

What makes a child throw himself down on the floor in an extreme temper tamtrum? It is the outgrowth of the crying-until-attention-comes experience. Why will a little girl defiantly fold her hands across her chest, sit back as far as she can in her highchair and refuse to eat nourishing food? She has learned that she can many times get her own way by working on her mother's already weary, nervous condition.

A young mother was observing her son in her backyard playing with a neighbor child. Unable to hear the conversations, she was shocked when she saw her son throw sand on his young playmate and then hit him in the face. She immediately ran to assist and comfort the injured and dirty boy, as well as to scold her own son.

"The Devil must have gotten into you," she said to him as she led him back into the house, "to make you throw dirt on that boy like that."

"Yea," the boy replied, "but it was my own idea to sock him on the kisser."

Remember the concept which you have been examining? It deals with repetition.

Do you recall reading "when there is a repetition of certain thoughts, certain actions follow. The repetition of those specific actions creates a habit. And the repetition of those habits creates an intricate part of your character"? If a child is impressed with certain thoughts over and over and over again, there is a very good chance that he or she will act on those thoughts. As an adult, "when your mind dwells on certain thoughts, you will eventually act on those thoughts. When you do that act many, many times, that act becomes an active habit. Repeating that habit many times will make that habit a "natural" part of your makeup; and therefore will play an important, if not leading, part in the development of what you actually turn out to be. In other words, it establishes your character."

Now the reason for the repetition of these undeniable facts is vital. The constant repetition of satanic impressions on certain minds eventually leads to their being worked out in and by those impressed lives. It is the general understanding that David Berkowitz was a prime candidate for murder through the influence of many an ordinary, sad childhood and youthful experience over which he had no control. Even his puberty's being slower than that of peers proved to be just another opportunity for satanic influences to find fertile ground in which to grow.

Satan sees, and reaches for, every opportunity to impress a human being that he or she is not as good as his or her friends, associates, neighbors, brothers and sisters, relatives, competitors, and even humanity in general. And once having established this belief deep in the mind, he is also able to impress individuals with ways to "show them." And the repetition of these ways will, in the majority of instances, bring about some inhuman act. Being able to impress them to carry out the act, he is generally also able to give that false sense of accomplishment, exhilaration, and "you-have-shown-them" sensation that will lead to more and worse acts of violence.

You can readily see where the impressions came from to shoot and kill the President of the United States in order to prove to a certain young actress that he was "somebody worthy of her love," can't you? Remember, also, the pulling of that gun's trigger did not come about when John Hinckley sat at a restaurant eating a grilled cheese sandwich. He did not think to himself [right then and there for the first time] "I'll go buy a gun and kill Ronald Reagen; then Jody Foster will really love me." His acts were the result of that slow and insidious assault on his subconscious mind by Satan.

Tennessee Ernie Ford sings so beautifully the hymn "His Hands." Yet, chances are excellent that he is not even aware of the full impact of the words that state that he is going back to the chapel in search of his Master's will. Those words are: "I've obeyed the wrong commands."

Now, think about something that will surely boggle your mind. Every thought you have ... every thought ... has one of two origins. Every thought is the direct and indirect product of one of two sources. You either think a good thought or a bad one. Every thought of love towards someone else has only one beginning. Every thought of hatred has but just one originator. When you think charitably about someone else, that thought is an impression on your mind by just one power. If you suddenly feel like "getting even" with someone, only one power put it there. Your thoughts are impressions from either a heavenly source or from a hellish one. There is no neutral ground, no half-way point, no impartial or unbiased territory.

Add to those sobering facts something else. You can control, to a great degree, which of these two powers dominate your thinking.

A few years back, a certain fad hit America. It began with commercial and professional long-distance truck drivers. They began to buy and use two-way radios called C.B.'s, or Citizen's Band Radios. Soon afterwards, millions of America's private automobiles were equipped with C.B.'s. Everyone began to learn and use the code language for communicating over these channels. Even though there was an ulterior motive by most of the purchasers [trying to find out where the radar-equipped police cars were located so as to not get a ticket for speeding], there was a certain degree of pleasure derived from carrying on conversations with other drivers.

When the number of C.B. radios increased to the place where almost one out of every five cars had them, even very short communications became very difficult, especially in and around large metropolitan areas. The common channel was 19. Channel 19 became so crowded with lots of people all trying to talk at the same time, that from time to time one driver could be heard telling another driver to "pick a clean channel." That is, they would turn to a channel no one was using, and carry on a conversation.

By the same token, it is very difficult, even for your Creator to communicate with you as He desires if your mind channels are all tied up. This is why Satan has worked so hard through these six thousand years to arrange things so that the average person is bombarded with every kind of conceivable influence, impression, sound, and sight that will jam the channels of the conscious [and subconscious] mind.

Your Creator communicated through clear channels to the apostle Paul and had him give this piece of advice to us today, "Finally, brethren, whatsoever things are true, whatsoever things are honest, whatsoever things are just, whatsoever things are pure, whatsoever things are lovely, whatsoever things are of good report . . . think on these things."

One of the most interesting experiments dealing with the influence of sound on the human mind came about in a laboratory where corn had been planted in the best of lighting, with

the finest soil and fertilizer. The corn was di-
vided into three groups. Each group was within
its own nearly soundproof areas, separated as
far as possible from the other groups. When
the corn was about one half of its full growth,
and all three groups reached this stage exactly
at the same time, a stereo speaker was placed
in one side of the glass cages the corn was
growing in.

Each glass cage had the speakers placed at
the exact same spot as the other cages. At the
specified time, each cage received a different
type of music through its own speaker. The
music was sent into each cage with the same
volume. The music was played for the same
period of time.

The first cage received "hard rock" music.
The second cage received classical music, and
the third inspirational and gospel music.

After two weeks, there was a decided change
in each cage. The corn in cage number one,
where the "hard rock" music was played, stopped
its normal growth at the exact height it had
reached when the experiment began. The corn
in cage number two, where the classical music
was being played, continued to grow. But, in
cage number three, where the inspirational and
gospel music was played, not only grew much
taller with a deeper and healthier green stalks,
the ears seemed to lean over closer to the
speakers!

Many people sincerely say, "Well, I just can't
seem to control what thoughts come to my
mind." Even though this is not altogether true,
a person can actually control its effects. As one
wise man said, "You can't keep the birds from

flying over your head, but you can sure keep them from building a nest there."

It has been proven, we are what we eat, and we are what we think. The Bible puts it this way, "As a man thinketh in his heart, so is he."

So, then, if we are surrounded by solid, helpful, healthy, clean, and inspiring people, places and things, then our chances of having solid, helpful, healthy, clean, and inspiring thoughts are excellent.

So, then, in order to insure that a man or woman can definitely ask for, and receive those needed electrical impulses to the brain which will give the correct impressions of what his or her talents, powers, and potentials are for true success and happiness, it can readily be seen that more will be required than simply asking the Creator one time.

And it is reasonable to assume that for proper communication certain locations, surroundings, and environments will make all the difference in the world.

Henry David Thoreau was a United States author and naturalist. His writings that advocate "nonviolent resistence to the state when it is unjust," have had great influence, even more so in this 20th century than when he wrote them in the middle 1800's. Mohandas K. Gandhi adopted many of Thoreau's ideas and named his movement for India's self rule after Thoreau's essay "Civil Disobedience."

Civil rights leader Martin Luther King, Jr., based his campaign of passive resistance on precepts found in the same essay.

Thoreau recognized that human beings need

to get away from the fast pace of life, and be able to just be quiet and think about things of real value. In "Walden," he wrote: "I went to the woods because I wished to live deliberately, to confront only the essential facts of life, and see if I could learn what it had to teach, and not, when I came to die, discover that I had not lived."

Possibly the two best times, [but not necessarily the only times], to start your program of seeking to find out what individual powers your Creator has instilled within you is very early in the morning and in the evening, before the mad rush of activities catch you up in the middle. When it is still dark and quiet, you can begin your day by asking God to truly impress you with what He would have you to do with your life, and then you can set the tone for your day's activities.

At night, when all of the clamor and mad rush has slowed and quieted down, when there is nothing to distract, you can truly concentrate on not only seeking those vital impressions, but also listening to hear them trying to zero in and picture them.

In the Old Testament there is the true story of a very powerful minister who had actually taken part in a supernatural demonstration. It seems as if everyone in his country had turned away from God and had begun to worship the sun. Even the king and his famous wife and the president and first lady, were taking off the words "In God We Trust." So, this minister made a nationwide notice that on a certain day, and at a certain place, he was going to present the most spectacular exposure of the government's fraud so the people could see how they had been victims of a "Firegate", instead of "Watergate."

This minister stood before most all of the citizens and asked God to send down fire to burn some monuments, or altars, that had been set up as part of their worship of the sun. Well, God did exactly what the minister had asked and it was spectacular in every way. He had proved that God does pay attention to His creatures.

Well, the queen was so angry at her being on "Sixty Seconds" [that was all it took for God to burn up the heathen altars], that she vowed to kill the minister within twenty-four hours. For some reason, the minister took off to hide in the mountains.

Once he got there, he took part in another audio-visual demonstration. Only this time it was designed for him ... and you and me. Standing on a ledge high up in the mountains, Elijah saw it all. First, a mighty windstorm hit the mountain so strongly that rocks were torn loose and fell down to the earth below. Elijah knew he was going to get a message from God. The Bible says, "But the Lord was not in the wind."

Elijah had not been back upon his feet too long before he felt the whole mountain start to quiver. It was an earthquake. Elijah held on with all his might. Now he knew for sure that he was going to hear God speak to him about his running from that wicked woman. "But," the Bible says, "the Lord was not in the earthquake."

All of a sudden, the sky became ablaze. Elijah

was almost blinded by the great balls of fire
that swirled around him. And as fast as the
fire came, it disappeared! The record reveals,
"But the Lord was not in the fire."

Then, the Bible indicates that after all the
mighty manifestations of divine power had
ended, there came to Elijah "a still small voice."
In the almost inaudible sound of a whisper,
God revealed His will to Elijah.

You got the point, didn't you? Elijah, like
you and me, had to have a clear channel, free
from the noise, busy rush, pressure, tension
and competitiveness of work at the office or
home, as well as from the off-duty and after-
work dash to parties, sporting events, movies,
amusement parks, and even the engrossing and
enrapturing television viewing. This is why
the Bible says, "Be still, and know. . . ."

If you are going to ask for, and receive, the
needed electrical impulses to your brain which
will give you the correct impressions of your
talents, not only must the channels of the mind
be cleared, and a concerted and concentrated
program of continually asking for those impressions be initiated, but something else is needed.

CHAPTER TEN
ZEROING IN

It has been said that "you can tell a man's or woman's age by those who are their heroes or heroines." In business, religion, sports, and the entertainment field heroes and heroines are always to be found. In the realm of sports, one man has kept his status as a hero for many years. His field is golf.

Although his golfing exploits have made him a giant in business, grossing several million dollars each year, there is still an excitement when he appears as a contestant in some tournament. His name, as you probably have already guessed, is Arnold Palmer.

Arnold Palmer has an outstanding record of success in professional golf. At one time in his career, there was virtually no one who could beat him. Even as a senior citizen today his ability to take that little white ball from tee to cup in a short number of strokes is tremendous. Yet, if you have ever played more than two or three games of golf, you could beat Arnold Palmer on any course in the world.

If you have played enough golf to be able to break the high score of 100 [keeping in mind

111

that professionals play in the realm of 60 strokes], you can still finish 18 holes with a lower score than Arnold Palmer. As a matter of fact, you could probably beat the finest golfer on the tour today!

By now, you have recognized that there is obviously a catch to it. Maybe the best score you have ever come into the club house with has been 90, and you know that you could never, ever come close to those huge money winners in golf. Well you are right and wrong. First, there is a catch to it. But, second, yes, you can not only come close, but you can beat those huge money winners in golf. Go back to Arnold Palmer, and let's arrange the scenario.

Since Arnold Palmer spends a lot of time in his Orlando, Florida home, the one who set up this challenge has selected a course in Central Florida, but one Arnold has never seen before.

Since you are nervous and had a hard time sleeping the night before, you go out to the driving range and hit about four buckets of balls. You have spent a long time on the practice putting green, and the time has come. Arnold comes into the club house with his caddy and a friend. You are introduced and your manager, who set it all up, decides that it is time to go out and put it to the test. Arnold stands up and says to his caddy, "Well, let's get this game going."

Before he can move, your manager jumps up and says, "Wait, Arnold, you have got to abide by these special rules for this experiment."

"What are they?" he asks with a smile.

"Just these two," the man says, "I'll have to put this dark handkerchief over your eyes. And, second, all your caddy can do is to hand you whatever clubs you select. He can't help you in any other way."

Of course, the experiment would be over, right then and there!

The reason you would beat Arnold Palmer would be the fact he could not see where he was aiming.

This ridiculous and fictional game may not be so ridiculous after all. Please get the point: in order for you to find complete and true happiness and success in this fast-fleeting life, it is essential to see where you are aiming!

It is true that in these professional classes where skilled and personable leaders spend time and energy in promoting self-improvement, they labor hard to get this point across. The major portion of any and all such seminars and lectures is spent on goal-setting. The greatest emphasis is placed on the absolute necessity of a goal before any type of success can ever be expected to be reached. As it has been said many times, a man without a goal is like a ship without a rudder. Do you know what is so tragic about a ship without a rudder? It is helpless. More than that, it is dependent on outside elements for reaching the shore. It cannot do anything about its situation. And that is basically what happens to a person without a goal. He or she has to depend on outside elements. They are at the whims of others. They drift aimlessly across the sea of life, being carried here and there against their will. They can do little about their situation in life.

A man was seen walking down a certain road at a very, very fast pace. One man with a

tremendous interest watched him walk about
two miles at this grueling speed. Finally, he
drove his car up alongside the man and looked
out to him as he maintained his pace.

"Where are you going?" he asked.

"I don't know!" he replied rapidly with short
breaths.

"You don't know where you're going?"

"No," he said again, "but I'm sure making
good time, ain't I?"

What good does it do a person if he beats a
fast pace to the grave, never having really
gone anywhere or done anything worthwhile?
Furthermore, what good does it do a man or
woman to drag out an aimless and non-pro-
ductive life?

It is not the quantity of years, but the quality of life that makes a person's time on planet
earth of any significance.

And there is no way, absolutely no way, for
a person to have that quality of life that makes
for true and complete happiness and success
without the Creator's conveying to that person
what his or her special talents, gifts, and powers are; and then that person aiming with all
his or her heart at the target those potentials
have placed before him or her.

You may attend, and participate in, a thousand self-motivation, self-improvement classes
where goal-setting is thoroughly explained as
well as thrillingly illustrated; and you may be
persuaded to determine what your goal is. But,
regardless of the time, energy and money ex-
pended in and on these clinics, classes, and
conventions, you will never know what your
true goal is until the One who set into your

brain the potentials of reaching that goal reveals just exactly what that goal is.

It was Oliver Wendell Holmes who said, "The great thing in the world is not so much where we stand as it is in what direction we are moving." And it is impossible to be going in the right direction without first getting the absolute correct directions.

You know now that you can definitely learn those directions you are to take in life so you can find true success and happiness. You know that in order to do this, it is absolutely essential to pray, pray often, and pray sincerely. You absolutely must ask God to give you unmistakable impressions and concrete conceptions. As you continue to place your petitions before Him, ideas will begin to form in your mind. The more you pray, the more these ideas will seem to begin to define themselves. As you keep asking Him to give you that clear picture, it will start to focus better, And as that picture sharpens more and more, something else begins to happen.

As these impressions start to narrow down to one specific area, you will find that you are actually picturing yourself doing just that very thing. You will also, without even realizing it at first, find yourself thinking of ways and means you could really be doing it.

You have heard of the "vicious cycle," haven't you? Well, at this point in your life, when you begin to contemplate how you could make that picture become a reality, a "victorious cycle" starts. The more you pray, the more impressed you become with your power and potentials in a particular project, profession, or after-retirement program. Then, the more impressed you become with that particular project, profession or program, the more you see it becoming a living and thrilling reality. And, the more you see yourself accomplishing it, the more you will pray!

Think about this next fixed fact very carefully:

The more your Creator fixes in your subconscious mind what your talents are, the more your subconscious mind will guide you to successfully using them. When you diligently apply this phenomenal principle, the impression you will get could very well become the reality of tomorrow.

But. . . .

The impression you get firmly fixed in your mind will be the exciting and rewarding reality of tomorrow, only when you put your total energy into making it become that reality. The impression, regardless of how deeply it becomes engraved in your mind, without your all-out effort, will never, ever be anything more than a dream.

Long ago, a salesmanager told one of his salesmen a little secret for success. That secret has been quoted and re-quoted until today it is one of the best formulas available. He simply said, "Plan out your work, and work out your plan."

Even after you have sincerely and persistently sought your Maker and He has started His repeated and ever-enlarging impressions of what you are to do in life, you have actually only just begun!

Once you firmly believe you have been given your "plan," then you need to devote your unflinching energy in working out your plan. And to succeed in that endeavor will require continued prayer, just as much as it did to get the knowledge of what your special work really is.

John Wanamaker was born near Philadelphia in 1838. At the age of 13, he worked as an errand boy. From 1857 to 1861, he was a paid secretary of the Y. M. C. A. In 1861, he and a brother-in-law went into the men's clothing business in Philadelphia. Wanamaker opened another store in 1869, just 8 years later. And again 8 years later, in 1877, he started a department store in an old freight depot. In 1869 he bought the Alexander T. Stewart department store in New York City. Wanamaker's fame is still known the world over.

John Wanamker said, "A man is not doing much until the cause he works for possesses all there is of him."

King Solomon put it this way, "Whatsoever thy hand finds to do, do it with all thy might."

Charles really loved and admired his father and must have spent much time trying to determine what he could do in life that would not only please his father [if his father could have known] but also be of real benefit to others.

His first job was a hard one, working for the New Haven Railroad for the massive sum of five dollars. Five dollars a week, not a day! Working diligently, he became a foreman for the railroad's power plant at Cos Cob, near Stamford, Connecticut.

Please note this very important fact: the highest weekly paycheck he ever received from the railroad was just under one hundred dollars.

Charles never married. By living very inexpensively, he began an amazing savings and investment campaign to get enough money for a special memorial to his father.

The development director of The University of New Hampshire confirmed these facts for this story. At eighty-one, Charles Stillings established a memorial scholarship in his father's name.

The amount of that scholarship fund was four hundred thousand dollars!

It has been said that when a man or woman finds his or her special work or project, and starts to put all he or she has into it, there comes an overwhelming transformation "like putting a 500-horsepower motor in a 10-year-old car."

There is a parable in the New Testament that Christ told which has been the source of rationalization for many people. They read the story and say, "Well, the rich get richer, and the poor get poorer." Actually, the parable gives several valuable lessons, and one in particular you might really benefit from if you are thinking more and more about giving this great concept a real try.

The parable tells that a rich man was getting ready to do a little traveling. He called three employees into his office, gave them notice of his forthcoming trip. Then he gave one employee five talents, another two, and the third one talent. They were told to go to work and see how they could increase their talents.

When he returned, he talked to the men to see how they had done.

The man who had received five talents had a

great big smile. He proudly explained how he had worked hard. Then he told of actually doubling the talents. The boss was truly pleased and gave him a bonus, as well as a real pat on the back.

The man who had been given two talents had just as big a smile as the first man when he walked into his boss's office. He had also worked hard and his talents were doubled, too. His boss congratulated him and promised a handsome reward.

When the third man came in, his head was hung low. There was a visible frown on his face. Apparently, he had not done very well. Immediately he began to explain why, "I knew thee that thou art an hard man, reaping where thou hast not sown, and gathering where thou has not strawed; and I was afraid, and went and hid thy talent in the earth. Lo, there thou hast that which is thine."

The Bible records what the employer thought of him. He was called "wicked and slothful [lazy]." Then the owner/manager called back the first man who had doubled his five talents and gave him the third man's one talent.

Don't dwell very long on the one man who failed. You see, he didn't even try. Think, however, of the joy and excitement that ran through the house that night when, after work, the first man told his wife and children all about his thrilling experiences that day. That happy family knew very well the old adage: "Success doesn't require any explanation, but failures have to be doctored with alibis."

One thing that Christ's parable teaches is that when you take what you have been given and use it with all your heart, mind, and energy, your talent will increase!

Another thing it teaches is that when you discover what you have been given in the way of talents and you do not use them to their fullest, you lose them. One of the greatest tragedies in life is the fact that many failures could have been turned into rich success if the people involved could have just made one more effort, tried one more time, or held on for just a few days, or even, minutes longer. A man or woman is never a failure until he or she accepts a closed door, a set-back, a hurdle, a disappointment, or a defeat as a permanent obstacle and gives up.

Your circumstances may not be ideal. They may even be bad. You may feel there is no way you can make anything out of your life in light of where you live, who your parents are, the small salary you or your mate may make, the heavy responsibility of a large family, your less-than-perfect health, your age, past small or large failures, non-supportive husband or wife, and etc, and etc. However, your circumstances can dramatically change when you discover your God-given goal and strive to reach it.

You see, it is impossible to be moving forward on the inside and the same time be standing still on the outside. And you just can't keep from having that inner-motion when you have the knowledge of exactly what the Supreme Being of all beings intends for you to do with your life.

As you may well know, the Old Testament portion of the Bible is written primarily in the

Hebrew language. The first time the Old Testament uses the word "vision" it comes from the Hebrew word "chazon." "Chazon" means "to perceive with inner vision." When you have persistently pleaded with your Maker to the place where you have that inner perception of your power and potentials, your planning begins, and, by His help, no one can keep you from fulfilling that plan!

No one, that is, except you!

Many successful counselors suggest that once you have zeroed in on your goal, you should never share it with anyone. Some individual succeeders will tell you that telling others of your plans can not only be dangerous, but devastating. Why?

Go back, in your mind, and recall the percentages that this book started with: 81% and 19%. You remember that the statistics show that only 19% of all the working force are happy with their goals and life. The remaining 81% are unhappy with no goals and totally unhappy with life.

That means, then, that if you talk with 100 people, 81 of them will be the wrong ones to discuss anything with, especially something as important as your future. In other words, the vast majority of human beings are totally incapable of passing on constructive suggestions and encouraging remarks.

Suppose you go into a hairstyling salon, sit down in one of the comfortable chairs, and as you are being cared for, the stylist notices that you are beginning to get some small bald spots on the back of your head. As the stylist continues to cut your hair, you get a ten minute sales pitch on a new and successful hair restorer. It all sounds very good and you are beginning to believe you should invest the $4.95 for a bottle and start treating those thin areas as soon as you get home.

Now, would you go ahead and purchase that bottle if, when the stylist leaves you for a moment to go and answer the phone, you notice as he walks in front of you that he has a huge bald spot in the back of his head?

Would you purchase and use diet pills highly recommended to you by an extremely obese pharmacist?

Would you listen attentively to a barefoot shoe salesman?

A young boy decided that in order to make money during his summer vacation, he was going to sell a special bottled iron tonic that gave him good commissions. One day, he saw some big men unloading watermelons out of a railroad car and onto a stake body truck. He took a bottle of the strength-building potion in his hand and climbed up onto the truck. The men, tired anyway, were eager for an opportunity to stop work, so they listened to his entire, enthusiastic sales pitch.

After he had finished, one man with bulging muscles looked down at his skinny frame and asked, "Do you take that stuff, son?"

"Why . . . ah, yes, yes I do!" he replied with the biggest smile he could produce.

"Well, then," the man replied, "I'm not going to buy any. I don't want what happened to you to happen to me!"

It has been said that for every person with a

good idea, there are a thousand others ready to tell him or her that it won't work.

Why ask advice from people who have failed? Why risk having the inner vision of your life ruined by others with no vision?

This is not to say that there are not good and solid people with whom you can discuss your plans constructively, but there is still a problem in that no one else in all the entire world can visualize what you visualize.

Before you ask anyone for his or her advice, think carefully about what great achievements he or she has performed that qualify him or her to set limitations for you. Remember, your impressions came from an infinite source who knows no failure.

CHAPTER ELEVEN
WHO'S KNOCKING

"What do *I* think?" Those four words are usually some of the most prized ones in our vocabulary because they are then followed by our own personal criticism of a concept, solution to a difficult situation, evaluation of an endeavor, or proposal to end a problem. And these are very seldom short conversations. Almost everyone is ready to give advice.

When you ask, however, for a definition of success, the answers are short and vague. And most are limited to four or five. One definition is a very short one, indeed, and seldom ever heard. As a matter of fact, it is just one word ... and a three-lettered one at that. Success can be defined by the word "n-o-w." That's right, "now!"

Get this: The Funk And Wagnalls Standard Dictionary of the English Language defines "now" almost as briefly as "now" defines "success." It simply says, "at once."

How, then, can "success" truly mean "at once"?

The answer lies in the antonym, the direct opposite, of "now," or "at once." The opposites would be, "later," "in the future," "not now," "by and by," "some time," "tomorrow," "someday," and etc.

Think of these opposites. They are positive and negative. "Not now," is a definite negative term, but look at how positive is the word "now!"

A group of friends came from many miles around a small Central Florida town to help build a metal warehouse. Their friend had discovered that if he were to ever fulfill his impression to go into a special type of inspirational publishing, it had to be "at once." Inspired by his dedication and energy, they volunteered their time and labor to work on the erection of the 24' × 60' building. One couple came about an hour after the work had begun. It was immediately obvious that this married pair were both athletic. When the husband's Marine Corp life was mentioned, it was not difficult to picture him marching a bunch of raw recruits and yelling at the top of his lungs. He and his wife both worked hard that day for their friend. And after everyone else had left, they stayed by to talk to the man whose venture they were both contributing to physically and morally.

They went into the house to sit down, rest, and drink some cold lemonade. And within a matter of a few minutes the handsome couple began to pour out their hearts to their friend. They, too, had an ever-increasing impression of what their life's work was to be. They felt that they were to work with men and women whose marriages were near the breaking point. They, through some difficult situations in their own marriage, had developed, or discovered, a very unique philosophy.

All of the volunteers that day had earlier spoken of his excellent singing talents. And it was no surprise that they believed they were to share their formula for a happy and healthy marriage through a combination of testimony and musical presentation. It was their desire to project to the audience their concept of true marital bliss by trial and error, heartache and heartbreak. Theirs was not an egotistical, but thrilling discovery that would make a real contribution to many people needing just such help. Then, they brought out their antonyms for "now."

The first big obstacle was finance. It seemed impossible to make payments on their home and operate some type of motor home life at the same time, especially just starting off as unknowns.

There was a deep obligation to their employer, who was not doing too well in his contracting business. If they were to leave him, the man's business might fold up.

There was the matter of brochures and advertisements. The brochures cost money and advertising did not, they thought, come free.

After a long period of many other antonyms, their friend asked, "Do you believe that this is what your Maker wants you to do?"

"Yes, we sincerely do," they both replied.

"Then," he asked, "if you believe that this is what your Maker wants you to do, do you also believe He [not you] is big enough to overcome any obstacles standing in your way?" They admitted, with heads lowered just a little bit and not looking at him in the eye any more, that He was definitely big enough to overcome any and all obstacles.

To their astonishment, their friend stood to his feet, looked them right in the eyes, and said, "Will you go right now to your boss and tell him that you are going to take on a special mission in life, one which he would approve and be proud ... and give him notice of your forthcoming resignation?"

They said, "Yes! We'll do it, right now!"

As they stood to their feet, he put his arms around this middle-aged couple, lowered his head and asked aloud for their Maker to honor their faith in Him, and to provide them with the wisdom and strength to carry out His will for their lives. Before they could realize it, he had headed them for the door and was pushing them out to their car to get going!

Within less than a month, they had their brochures, and had held one concert in a nearby large city. The audience appreciatively gave them a contribution to help them on their way. They also sold some tapes and records they had made long before but had not done much with in the way of sales.

Arrangements were made so that their father could handle all the correspondence channeled through his address for bookings and etc. They left for their Michigan home with several bookings in hand.

Since that time, which was not long ago, they have held concerts and shared their secrets for successful marriages in such far off places as Hawaii and England! Their letters to their friend back in Florida are enthusiastic testimonies to the fact that when the Creator finally gets through to His creatures, and those creatures recognize their powers and potentials and set out to fulfill those dreams and impressions, the Creator gives them just a little boost along their upward climb.

Chances are excellent that Jim and Yvonne Chamness would still be dreaming about "someday" helping others find meaning in marital life if they had not decided to start making their dreams come true "at once." They are encouraging many people to try to have a truly happy marriage and successful life through their testimony in word, music, and song. And it all began when they decided to do it "now."

A dream, an inspiration, an impression of your goal is a wonderful thing only if you work to make it come true. By the same token, a beautiful vision of your particular potential is a tragedy, a nightmare, if it never goes beyond the gray matter. "One day" can become "never," if you procrastinate, put off, making your plans become a reality. And it is just that, putting off plans, which leads the majority of individuals to fall into that 81% catagory. Procrastination destroys so many lives that it should be classified as a hideous crime.

Another term that should be banned from use by human beings is the one that goes like this, "It's almost too late to start anything like that." You hear its second cousin all the time, "I'm just too old to do something like that."

These words of procrastination could actually be termed curse words. You see, when your Creator finally impresses you with a vision of your unique talent and special potentials, and you say, "Well, maybe someday, but I just can't see how I can do it now," or throw in a "later," or a "not now," in all probability, you will never, ever even begin to make that talent or potential become a thrilling reality. That, friend, is very close to being profane or sacrilegious. Your Maker shows you what you are to do in life and you reject Him by your disbelief and procrastination.

When a person comes to the awareness of his or her powers, begins to make plans and programs to see those powers come alive and grow to their fullest potentials, there comes a sense of closeness to the Creator that is almost unbelievable. And that almost unbelievable closeness is what He wants you to have, and that is why He will give you an understanding of what you are to do in life to achieve fulfillment, joy and satisfaction.

Suppose you are a mother. You have a daughter you love dearly. One day, you decide to surprise her with a beautiful dinner. Just after she leaves for senior high school, you start preparing that fabulous meal . . . make a special trip to the super market, stop by a friend's and borrow a big Bundt pan your daughter admired. You even do a little research through several large recipe books.

Since your husband's fatal heart attack, there are just the two of you now. You really want to spend some time with your daughter this evening, and this meal will really set the stage for that mother-daughter talk.

After spending the major portion of the day in the kitchen, you have time to take a quick shower, change clothes, and place the meal on the table before she comes in from her after-school band practice.

Hearing her come in the door, your heart skips a beat, and you call, "I'm in the dining room."

She comes in, smiles at you, looks over the meticulously beautiful table setting and says, "I'm not hungry. I'm going to go to my room and go to sleep. I'm just bushed."

"But, Honey," you plead, I've worked all day making this meal. I so hoped we could spend some time together. I really want to talk over some important things with you."

She turns, walks towards her room, and says, "Not now, Mom, we'll talk some other time." And, of course, the vital discussion never takes place.

Suppose that you are a father. You have just one son. He has just graduated from high school. You recognize in your son so many fine and admirable talents. He is personable, nice looking, in good physical condition and has made good grades all through school. To you, he has all the potentials of a real leader.

You have asked him to go off for a weekend trip. You have a special place in mind. You have made arrangements to have use of a friend's mountain hide-a-way that is isolated from almost everything. So, the two of you make the long hike up the hill, loaded down with all the necessities for the three days and two nights. The cabin is surprisingly clean, so little time is spent away from fishing and relaxing.

The afternoon you plan to leave for home, you ask your son to take a walk with you. The two of you go to a smooth ridge overlooking the winding river way, way below you. The scenery is breathtaking. And there is nothing said for a few minutes as you both just breathe in the fresh air and scan the fabulous picture before you.

Then, after the deadly silence is broken by the call of a large bird, you look at your son and say, "I've brought you up here for a special reason. I've been doing a great deal of thinking about your future. I see in you so many fine characteristics of a truly successful man. I feel that it is time for us to discuss your plans."

He kicks off his shoes, leans back against the rock and replies, "Well, Dad, I've already worked out a plan for my life."

You are pleased and tell him so. "Well, what are your plans?"

"I've decided that I'm not going to college. I have this friend, Tom, and we see so many things the same way. And we're going to go live in a railroad boxcar that's in the rear of his uncle's old junk yard down on Demasse Street. His uncle will let us stay there free just so someone will be on the premises to scare off any prowlers. We won't have to worry about food 'cause we've got another friend, Tony, who says we can have all the left-overs from his restaurant if we'll just bring down a bucket and take it home. We just want to get out of the rat race, Dad."

Chances are excellent that if you were either this mother or father, your heart would be broken. What about your Creator? How does He feel after doing so much to give you the powers and potentials for a full and successful, truly happy life, if you reject them, much less even attempt to discover what those powers and potentials are? How does He feel, after you do understand them, you keep putting off implementing them?

The old adage that "opportunity only knocks once," may not necessarily be true. But in the majority of cases, when it does "knock" the first time and no one opens the door, it doesn't have much of a desire to return and "knock" again.

But by the same token, history shows that when it does "knock," and an enthusiastic and appreciative man, woman or young person invites it in, "opportunity" does seem to be magnetically drawn back to that same man, woman or young person to "knock" some more.

As you know, a magnet has two forces, two powers. It does draw, to be sure, but it also repels. Can you run the risk of repelling "opportunity" by not throwing open your doors when it "knocks?"

Despite the fact that H. Ross Perot is a billionaire [not millionaire, but billionaire], many people never heard of him until he became actively engaged in a campaign to free the P.O.W.'s [the prisoners of war] in Vietnam. The Texas based electronics man chartered two Boeing 707's to take Christmas presents and necessities to those prisoners. His financial growth is a sensational story in itself. "Opportunity" "knocked" at his doors many times. Do you think "opportunity" would have made its repeated "knocks" if Ross had repelled it when it came "knocking" in Texarkana, Texas when he was twelve years old?

The Texarkana Gazette paid a commission to its young paperboys who delivered the paper to their customers' doors. It is believed that the commission was 30%. It seems that there was a difficult and long route that not too many boys wanted. It was in the black community. Ross went to the circulation manager [the one who worked directly with the paper route boys] and made him a proposition. He said he would take the black route for 70%. It was agreed upon, maybe because no one else wanted the route, and maybe because the manager did not think he would last long on that hard route. Ross delivered his papers on horseback and made a success.

There is a definite, undeniable, relationship between his early success as a horseback-riding, paperboy and his amazing achievements today.

Another young man, age sixteen, proved that it's dangerous at any age to procrastinate. While working as a delivery boy, he was struck by a car in Memphis, Tennessee. This constituted his having to wear a body cast for a year. His mother worked so hard to pay his bills as well as for the necessities of their home that she became ill and was hospitalized. Therefore, this seventeen year old young man had to withdraw from school and provide for her, too.

"Opportunity" "knocked" when he discovered that a certain man had a popcorn machine he was not using. He purchased the machine for the grand total of $50.00. However, his sincerity and need coupled with his persuasion, allowed him to get it for just $1.00 per week.

He rented a small space in a theatre, and began selling hot popcorn to those coming in and out of the movies. He made so much money that he was evicted, and the theatre began selling its own popcorn [with his machine he sold to them for . . . $50.00].

If that young man had put off his impressions, and had taken the typical job offered high school drop-outs, you might never, ever had experienced staying in a Holiday Inn. That young popcorn vendor was Kemmons Wilson, the founder of Holiday Inns!

With a clear, heaven-sent, impression of your powers and potentials as a result of sincere and persistent praying, with a determination that through His help you are going to see those impressions become successful fulfillments, and with that special, added decision to do it "now," or "at once," "opportunity" will be "knocking" at your door many times.

CHAPTER TWELVE
AND NOW

In 1903, when very little was known about the electrical current in the nervous system, one extremely perceptive individual wrote this enlightening statement:

"The brain nerves that connect with the whole system are the medium through which heaven communicates with man [kind]."

You have been examining this concept, looking at living proof of its validity and exciting power. And, unless there is some type of short-circuit in your own brain nerves, you have been challenged to make this concept become an exciting and rewarding experience in your own life.

You now understand that your Creator definitely placed within you certain undeniable and individual powers, talents, gifts, and potentials.

You also recognize that, like any sincere and loving parent wants only the best for his or her children, your Maker wants you to come to a true and vivid awareness of your talents.

You realize that you can actually reach the place in your life where you can have that clear and concise conception, and that it will come about only by communicating with your Creator.

You know that this communication will never, ever become a realistic two-way experience until you first engage in sincere and persistent prayer.

You are now aware of the tremendous fact that once His will for your life is clearly presented to you and you have a real dream of true success, you must do all within your power to carry out His will or that dream will become a nightmare.

You have grasped the gripping truth that to truly carry out His will for your successful and fulfilling life, you cannot possibly procrastinate, put off, doing His will. There has to be that unflinching determination that you must do it "now."

You are also convinced that by your acting "at once" on your clear, heaven-sent impressions [once they are firmly imbedded in your mind as coming from God], your success and happiness will increase with each carrying out of His will for your life. In other words, that long sentence says that you know that "opportunity" will "knock" and "knock" again as you do all you can, with His help, to enthusiastically and appreciatively throw open those doors.

And you can now conceive of the fact that success may come in your life in stages, and not necessarily all at once.

Remember reading about how the enemy of your life has worked so successfully to keep mankind from coming to an awareness of God-given powers and talents? You will recall how this mastermind has caused every individual person on planet earth to have what is termed an "inferiority complex." When you read those facts, and came to the realization that he has swindled you and millions of others, out of a lot of joy, peace of mind, success and real fulfillment in life, it sort of made you a little mad, didn't it?

A certain man came to this understanding about twenty some odd years ago. When he did, it changed his life. It led him into years of personal research work into other areas where the arch-enemy might be keeping mankind from enjoying more of these God-given gifts.

And what he discovered is absolutely even more amazing!

When he had been able to document his findings, he began to get certain, increasing electrical impulses to his brain. He began to experience a repetition of one particular impression. The repetition led him to do a great deal of communicating with his Maker. And those communications brought him to the place where he was convinced of what He wanted him to do in his life.

He became so deeply impressed with this heaven-sent program, that he and his wife decided that in order to have peace of mind and any semblance of a normal life, they were to follow those impressions. You see, his wife, too, did an equal amount of communicating with her Maker so as to make sure that her husband's impressions were coming from above!

It seems that the impressions they both received were to share with the world this additional area of life in which Satan had once

again prevented the majority of human beings
from understanding. This sharing was to be
done in the form of a book. This book was to
challenge the readers to look behind the scenes,
to delve just a little deeper, and to investigate
more before reaching definite conclusions in
that one vital area.

Since the husband had difficulty spelling
"dirt" without getting it on his hands, authoring
a book seemed an impossibility. But, there was
that definite and compelling impression to do
it. So, they took a leave of absence from their
work, sold their home, took out their savings,
and went to a quiet area of the United States
to try to write that book.

His personal research to try to determine if
man's arch-enemy had also tricked him in other
areas brought him first to wonder what many
people are puzzled over, too. That is, "Why are
there so many different denominations in existence today?"

Protestants, Catholics and Jews will all agree
in the teaching of a Supreme Being Who created planet earth as well as its solar system.
They all are in harmony over the fact that that
Supreme Being is God. They understand that
He is sinless and holy, and that He did communicate personally with his first created beings
on an one-to-one, face-to-face, basis only up
until they sinned. This sin created a barrier
between God and man. That led to the formation of a different type of common communication for the masses of human beings now living
on a sin-stained planet. God, then, led His creatures into the writing of regulations and in-
structions from God to man for man's happiness

and success. That written communication, of course, is the Bible. Through His electrical impulses to the brains of many men from many different walks of life, the communication became a reality.

Think about this puzzling dilemma. Today, in a modern, 20th Century, advanced society, we have one God, one book from God to man, and over two hundred and fifty different denominations declaring all kinds of different doctrines about certain basic facts!

How can there be one code book and several hundred diverse interpretations? Two plus two equals four, regardless of how many people would try to state otherwise. Surely, with one code book, one set of rules and regulations, one distinct formula, there can only be one correct teaching of those facts.

This particular man's research brought him to the awareness of the fact that there are only about eighteen basic segments making up the sum total teachings of the Bible. That is, the Bible contains just about eighteen basic doctrines. It is a fact that you can elaborate on those basic doctrines or teachings in many, many different ways, but they stay the same number. There had to be a simple explanation for all the confusion.

In his search for the answer, he discovered that there was far more to the arch-enemy's bringing on all the confusion through many different churches so that mankind would be overwhelmed by all the different teachings. Slowly, he began to unfold what can easily be called one of the most sinister schemes ever conceived. And this scheme is actually swindling millions of sincere men, women and young people everywhere!

He was stunned almost beyond belief as he saw this world-wide hoax going on which is defrauding millions. As he saw more and more of this diabolical deception, it seemed impossible to have ever been conceived, much less being carried out with astonishing success.

And here was this man who had discovered these astonishing things compelled to write about it, and he had never written anything in his life except a letter or two, and some of them came back with "unable to deliver" stamped on them. So, needless to say, he and his wife communicated more than ever with their Maker for wisdom in presenting these shocking facts. They wanted to be able to share these astounding events with everyone without anyone's getting offended. They became convinced that that was an impossible task. So, they decided to pray diligently for the words to write, and leave the success up to the One who communicated with them.

The couple prayed long and hard for the ability to convey to others that they, too, like themselves, had been swindled, and yet not have the reader become turned off before examining all the facts. After all, no one likes to realize that he or she might have been taken in, especially in the realm of religion.

The author even considered not putting his name on the book. This way, no one might consider him as another writer on an ego trip. However, in order to give credence to these facts, he would not be able to use a pseudo

name. His name would have to be on the cover
as well as inside the book.

After almost one long year of diligent and
frustrating work, the book was produced. To
attract the would-be-reader's attention, it was
decided to have a bright red background on the
cover. At the top, in white script letters, the
driving force behind the book is seen: "At Last,
The Documented Story Of A World-wide Hoax
Defrauding Millions ... [Maybe Even You!]"

Near the middle of the cover, and beneath
those white script words, was a yellow sun-
burst with flaming edges portraying the sun
burning through the cover. In green letters
these words blare out" Discover The Swindle
Of All Swindles Being Done ALL IN THE
NAME OF THE LORD." [And the last seven
words make up the title: ALL IN THE NAME
OF THE LORD].

It seemed almost too bold to tell the person
picking up, and looking at the book that he or
she might have been swindled in the religious
realm, so on the back cover, these explanations
were given:

"DISCOVER the world's greatest fraud as it
unfolds from creation to this present date.

"SEE the inside story of how Satan has succeeded in selling his counterfeit teachings to
almost the entire world.

"LEARN about the conglomerate of religious
organizations who help bring about earth's last
conflict."

At the bottom of the back cover there is an
additional challenge which reads:

"Now you can discover for yourself what has
puzzled millions for centuries!"

Remember, all these startling declarations and challenges were printed in red, yellow, green, black and white colors which almost jump off the page.

By the descriptions you have just read, what would you think were the chances of such a book becoming a success? Would it ever sell the first copy?

Well, by the time you read this, that one book will have been reprinted five times! It not only has had a national circulation, it is being translated in two additional languages!

And all of this has come about without the normal channels of "publisher to distributor, distributor to wholesaler, wholesaler to retailer, and retailer to consumer."

The reason for the departure from these normal marketing channels was that in order to get the kind of distribution they felt was necessary, the author and his wife also published and distributed the book themselves.

In addition, their newly-founded firm has published four other books with equally successful circulation. Three of the other books have also been reprinted ... and all in less than three years!

If you could read the almost daily letters this husband-wife publishing team receive from men, women and young people, thanking them for not only enlightening their minds, but encouraging their lives, you would know why they believe wholeheartedly in the concept that true success and fulfillment in life only come when a man, woman or young person determines to learn and follow God's will for their lives.

This concept is working for them. It is working for others. It will work for you!

As you carry out this sensational and life-altering concept in your own life, you will discover that it is far more exciting and rewarding than any adjectives and superlatives could convey to you. Now, it is all up to you. And it is all up to you to begin "at once" to GO UP!

* * *

You may not have been aware of the fact that two certain words are almost completely missing in all of the pages you have read thus far in this book. With just a few exceptions they are used only in quotations and in quoting others. They have been left out for a very vital reason.

Those two words are "we" and "our".

These personal pronouns have been deliberately omitted so that nothing would prevent you from coming to the thrilling understanding of this tremendous concept. It is especially so in the true story of the husband and wife publishing team.

You see, that team consists of Bill and Dee Stringfellow. It seemed essential for you to have no personalities be seen in these pages. This was done so that you could come to a full understanding of this sensational concept without trying to draw a mental picture of the authors as most readers do.

Now, please allow us to depart from the rigid refusal to use these personal pronouns.

You have read about the formation of our publishing company and the amazing foundation on which it was built. We believe that it would be a real injustice to you to describe the amazing book in which these explosive discoveries are grippingly shared with the reader and not invite you to learn them for yourselves. They could very well be even more of a challenge than those facing you in this present book. They could very well be the most amazing concepts you ever read.

ALL IN THE NAME OF THE LORD is a 172 page paperback book described over and over again by individuals writing us as "something I could not get out of my mind . . . I just could not put the book down until I had finished it." You, too, will find it very difficult to put down once you begin reading it.

In order to help you get your own personal copy "at once," you will find a special coupon on the next page. The retail price of this book is $2.95. However, if you fill out the coupon "now," and get it in the mail "right away," your book will be sent to you for just $2.50 [and we will pay all postage and handling charges].

As you read the astounding book ALL IN THE NAME OF THE LORD, and as you start your quest to have God's will for your life working in your life, as outlined in this book, you will have only one thing to do. That is, to GO UP!